POINT OF VIEW DESIGN BY JAY SPECTRE

POINT OF VIEW
DESIGN BY JAY SPECTRE
WITH GEOFFREY N. BRADFIELD

INTRODUCTION BY PAIGE RENSE

A Bulfinch Press Book   Little, Brown and Company   Boston Toronto London

Endpapers:
A Spectre fabric,
"St. Mark's Square,"
after a fourteenth-century
Venetian mosaic.

First Edition

Library of Congress Cataloging-in-Publication Data

Spectre, Jay.
     Point of view: design by Jay Spectre/Jay Spectre with Geoffrey
Bradfield; introduction by Paige Rense.— 1st ed.
        p.   cm.
     "A Bulfinch Press book."
     ISBN 0-8212-1849-2
     1. Spectre, Jay—Themes, motives. 2. Interior decoration—United
States—History—20th century. I. Bradfield, Geoffrey. II. Title.
NK2004.3.S68A2 1991
729 .092—dc20
                                                              91-2959

Bulfinch Press is an imprint and trademark of Little, Brown and Company (Inc.)

Published simultaneously in Canada
by Little, Brown & Company (Canada) Limited

Designed by Rick Horton

Typography by Hamilton Phototype

Printed and bound by Everbest Printing Co. Ltd.

PRINTED IN HONG KONG

For John E. Reid III

ACKNOWLEDGMENTS

I cannot begin to thank anyone without first acknowledging the enormous debt of gratitude due Paige Rense, editor in chief of *Architectural Digest*, not only for her introduction to this book, but also for generously granting permission to use photography from the *Architectural Digest* archives that was crucial to this book.

I wish to give special thanks to my partner, Geoffrey Bradfield, without whom this book would not have happened.

Thanks to the staff at Bulfinch Press/Little, Brown, especially Carol Leslie, publisher, and our editor, Lindley Boegehold, who with Dana Goodall cheerfully fueled us with support, and all of those who extended early encouragement.

I would like to thank my assistant, Meredith Nieves, for coping with the follow-up details, and my staff for their support.

For their generous involvement I wish to thank Buck Shuford, president of Century Furniture; our other licensees; and Carl Levine, senior vice president of Bloomingdale's, for his professional advice and friendship.

This book could never have been realized without the very generous cooperation of my wonderful clients, who allowed us into their houses and apartments: to them I extend my warmest thanks. And to Robin Roberts, president of Clarence House, who had the courage earlier on to respond to my creative challenge.

Thanks to all of the photographers, Durston Saylor, Peter Vitale, Jaime Ardiles, Mary Nichols, Mark Ross, Robin Bowman, Bob Grant, and Nancy Rica Schiff, and their assistants for providing the visual material in this book. Thanks to Rick Horton for designing the book, and thanks to Glenn Harrell for organizing the words to express the visual images.

I know I have left out many individuals and companies, so I would like to extend a blanket thanks to these people (some of whom do appear in the picture credits).

Jay Spectre

CONTENTS

POINT OF VIEW DESIGN BY JAY SPECTRE

INTRODUCTION

The interiors of our rooms reveal our personal interiors. Ourselves laid bare. There for all to see. So we want to be safe. Safe from what? Judgment. Whose judgment? Others'. Those ominous Others. Will they heap ridicule upon us? Will they find us guilty of bad taste and sentence us to Social Oblivion? Surely they will. But wait. We may yet be saved. A decorator may arrive with a reprieve. And if we are fortunate it will be Jay Spectre.

He may enter tap-dancing. If he does, pretend it's perfectly natural. And it is because Jay has always believed he is really Fred Astaire. Let's take it from the top. They have a lot in common. Style. Grace. Creativity. Innovation. Complexity of talent. And Jay, too, makes it look easy. He comes into a room and choreographs the basics. Taps in the details. Twirls the fabrics. Jazzes with contemporary riffs. Composes a medley of antiques. Swings with art.

Suddenly, without even knowing how it happened, you're dancing. You're Ginger Rogers. Or Gene Kelly. You're a better dancer than you ever thought possible. First Jay led and you followed. Then he showed you some old steps and some new steps. He swung into the rhythm. You picked up. And there you are. Dance partners. Baby, take a bow. You have it. A Jay Spectre design.

Take it from me. I've been watching my friend Jay dance for over twenty years. I have shown his work thirty-one times. We met not long after he arrived in New York City from Louisville, Kentucky, with more determination and talent than most well-established designers. I've watched the talent and the man grow apace, strengthen, refine, become more sure, more authoritative. He exerts his authority quietly, like the Southern gentleman he is. But quality is nonnegotiable, and for a good reason: He can't work any other way. The attention to detail must be there, even if it's not apparent to the casual eye. Jay understands the importance of detail, and so will you because he will show you. With Jay it's not just a word. It's his professional standard. He builds on a solid foundation or he doesn't build at all. He won't dance, why should he? He won't dance, how could he? He won't dance, my dear, with you— or anyone else, if he can't lead. He should lead and we should follow, because the man knows where he's been and where he's going, as you will see in the following pages of *Point of View: Design by Jay Spectre.*

Paige Rense
Editor in Chief
Architectural Digest

The Loews United Artist Theater, Louisville, Kentucky, a while back. The theater is dark, and Jean Harlow is slinking through a glorious all-white Art Deco room. The movie theater is furnished in grand American cinema style: lavish velvet draperies, gilded chairs, a ceiling like the sky with stars that twinkle and clouds that move. Sheer magic on screen and in the mind of the young Jay Spectre, absorbing every curve, every textile, every detail.

Inspiration is like love. Sometimes you have to go to extremes to get it and sometimes it comes very easily.

"I found it at the movies," says Jay Spectre without a moment's hesitation. "Style, glamour, sex. In short, a world I've never stopped dreaming of." The glorious black-and-white sets of old Hollywood films from the thirties held Spectre captive as a child at the neighborhood picture palace every Saturday afternoon. "It never occurred to me while I was sitting in the dark watching shadows dance across the screen that they would influence the rest of my life. To me there was — and is — nothing more glamorous than the sets for Fred Astaire and Ginger Rogers: those shiny black floors, that white woodwork and drapery."

The celluloid depiction of Art Deco — marvelous in movies like *Dinner at Eight*, *Our Dancing Daughters*, *The Divorcee* — was Spectre's main exposure to the style. "The B-picture nightclub settings looked up-to-date to me," he says. "In those days Art Deco interiors were not nostalgic, they were very modern. Hollywood used modernist architecture and decoration to define a certain personality, very often an international type, a gangster, or an independent woman."

1.
SPECTRE VISION
..

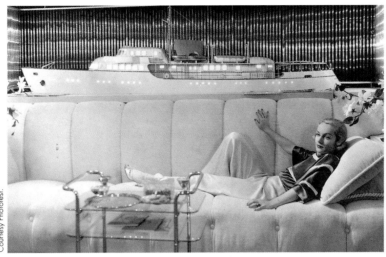

Courtesy Photofest.

Carole Lombard with perhaps the inspiration for the channeled sofa.

SEDUCED BY THE SILVER SCREEN

L E F T
Anders Randolph
and Greta Garbo in
The Kiss (1929).
A classic Art Deco
movie set.

The look that emerged in the Roaring Twenties and was eclipsed by World War II drew from the era's avant-garde art movements, including Cubism, Futurism, the Bauhaus, the International school. Its hallmarks were a fascination with the newest materials as well as the finest, an exoticism derived from the cultures of the Orient and Africa, an emphasis on technology and the machine. It was this century's self-indulgently sumptuous style. "Life had a newness, a style, and a naïveté that does not exist today," says Spectre. He recalls his first trip to Radio City Music Hall, America's Jazz Age monument: "It is one of the most exciting places I've ever been. To think it was created in this century!" Spectre's wonder at the accomplishments of this century has not diminished in the intervening years.

"My sense of style and taste developed out of a desire to know how people lived," says Spectre. "I wanted to find out what good taste was. I wanted something that would take me where I had never been."

In search of this something, Spectre set out for Europe aboard an ocean liner in 1954 at the age of twenty-five; he says he was ready to go at eleven. The ship's design reinforced his love affair with streamlining, so much a part of the Art Deco aesthetic embraced by Hollywood. But he responded to more than its luxurious associations; the true economy of design realized in staterooms, automobiles, zeppelins, rail cars continues to fascinate and inspire him. Not that Spectre wants to repeat the twenties and thirties any more than he does the eighteenth century. We must tailor our environments to the way we live today.

Spectre woke up to being a visual person when he was in Europe on that first trip.

5

"There is nothing quite equal to your first experience abroad, to the first time you see Paris or Rome. I grew aware of what the world was and what beauty was about, like walking down the street and discovering a fountain that was designed by Michelangelo, or like learning to appreciate the integrity of a seventeenth-century building.

"When I was a young man, a New York designer asked me in a very arrogant way where I went for inspiration in Louisville. Except for the movies, I had never been anywhere for inspiration. I didn't know what he meant until I had been to Paris."

Evolution of a Style

Alfred Hitchcock once said that style is a form of self-plagiarism. It is repeated and reinterpreted again and again. If so, the Jay Spectre style begins in the New York City apartment he designed for himself in 1968. It is a far cry from the period rooms he had been doing in his native Kentucky, where he operated a decorating business and an antiques import shop. "I had really been a traditionalist up until then," says Spectre. "But I was hell-bent on making a statement. I liked being creative and innovative, and I liked being in New York. I wanted to be noticed."

The new look Spectre created, based on functional opulence articulated with high-tech materials, has since become his trademark. It worked. "I really believed in the look I was developing. What the city needed least, I felt, was another decorator who could do a pretty French or English interior."

When Spectre first saw the East 57th Street apartment at the urging of his friend Robin Roberts, president of Clarence House, he was not overly impressed. "My idea of a New York apartment was something high up with a great view and a fireplace and all the fantasy you envision moving to this city," says Spectre. "This one had none of those things, but it did have space and it was available. I just somehow felt impetuous enough to take it."

Spectre set to work transforming the rented space — two bedrooms, a terrace, and a small kitchen with a window — into a home and office for himself. In the completed interior we see a definite passion for texture, a talent for mixing objects of different provenances and styles, a willingness to take risks.

Two goals — to give the apartment a much-needed sense of architecture and to make the eight-foot ceilings appear higher — were accomplished with the novel sheathing of the living room and entrance hall walls with corrugated metal. It gave the appearance of armor. "I found someone to do it for me in the yellow pages," says Spectre, who loves the gleam and glamour of all metals. "I used galvanized steel for the bookshelves and vertical blinds, the first that were used residentially. This was before there was a Levolor company." Friends told him they now knew how it felt to be a sardine in a tin can.

Spectre reintroduced a color of the thirties, a deep aubergine, on the ceilings. The wooden floors were stained a very dark Cordovan brown, concealed in part by an antique Bessarabian rug. The sofa and chairs were upholstered in cognac-colored leather. For tables, Spectre used a Giacometti coffee table and a marble bakery counter from a Parisian pâtisserie.

A little fantasy is something Spectre thinks no one should live without. In this environment it was a touch of the psychedelic: An artist's

TOP RIGHT

The living room in Spectre's first Manhattan apartment, lined in controversial corrugated metal, with Spectre's signature mix of contemporary and antique.

BOTTOM RIGHT

The library, also lined in metal, with galvanized steel bookcases. An innovative juxtaposition of textures: leather, metal, and glass.

installation flashed colorful images of abstract paintings on the louvered blinds.

The master bedroom was as striking as the living room. Instead of radical steel or something mundane like wallpaper, Spectre opted for mirror on the walls and ceiling, an Art Deco treatment he had admired in the movies. He chose vertical blinds of galvanized steel for the windows again and industrial gray carpeting. Pedestals of opaque industrial glass, ''the kind used for factory windows,'' were lighted from within to form glowing supports for a collection of pre-Columbian art. ''The pedestals served as the lighting for the room and created a dramatic mood,'' says Spectre. A surprise was the inclusion of a Louis XVI bed with distressed white paint in this slick setting. Unusual pairings — here the juxtaposition of the handcrafted and the high-tech — is vintage Spectre.

The imaginative daring the young designer exhibited in this apartment had its roots in earlier decorating projects in Louisville. Spectre recalls in vivid detail his first job (he was only eighteen), a cottage in Frankfort, Kentucky. Inspired by the brown-and-pink packaging of an Hermès box, he painted the walls of the master bedroom dark chocolate and did the draperies in pale pink and the floors in celadon carpeting. ''I have always loved challenges,'' says Spectre. ''Here I tried to do something that would be flattering to a beautiful lady with white hair. Let me tell you, the dark walls were very new. Black was my first idea, but then I thought, 'She can't handle it.' You know you can't push your clients too far.''

Spectre's second home for himself was a country retreat he built in 1971 to escape the hustle and bustle of city living. He commissioned architect Harry Bates to design a small modern brick and tinted-glass structure, "one of the first indoor-outdoor houses in the area," according to Spectre, on a densely wooded property near Southampton on Long Island's eastern shore. Bare windows in the connected living and dining areas, which soar to eighteen feet, open up the interior to the garden; the more private spaces, the bedrooms and kitchen, are secluded. "I tried to make the walls disappear into the background by painting them all the same deep chocolate brown." The one exception is the black sculpture-clad wall specially created by Spectre's friend, the artist Louise Nevelson. "The sculpture, which she signed J-A-Y in the corner as a surprise, was assembled for me by Louise from older pieces from a show that she did for the Whitney a few years before. Louise wanted me to have a Nevelson living room. It was the only piece of art I had in the room. She selected the paint color and blue lights that washed the wall and the sculpture. It was tremendously dramatic." Throughout the house, the materials are consistent too: natural black slate for the floors, the dining table, the kitchen and bathroom counters, and vertical wood planks for the walls. "It was like a spaceship in the woods compared to its shingled neighbors," says Spectre. "But at that time I wasn't really aware of a Southampton look, and if I had been, I wouldn't have followed it anyway. Ignorance is not only bliss; I've come up with some great ideas in the absence of formal knowledge."

The living room sofas upholstered in camel-colored leather are a relief from the darkness of the slate and paint. Spectre dreams up his designs in black and white, before

The dramatic exterior facade of Spectre's country retreat in Southampton, LI, showing the serene relationship between architecture and nature.

ABOVE

Sophisticated brushed-steel guest room furniture with swiveling nightstands—a Spectre prototype.

RIGHT

An international mix of objects and furniture with a backdrop of the dramatic Louise Nevelson wall.

"colorizing" them. Crucial in his mind are form and function; finishes and colors can be adjusted for what amounts to very much the same final product. Here, the decorative interplay involves tonal values, mass, and texture, in a more cinematic vein. "The house didn't need color," says Spectre. "I always had fresh flowers and I let the lush outside take care of the rest."

Spectre made use of metal again — in the guest room furniture of brushed steel, the master bedroom's media wall unit in polished steel, and the sleek dining room chairs. "I've always liked steel furniture, whether it's eighteenth century or contemporary," says Spectre. He outfitted the guest room with swiveling nightstands set with electronic controls to activate the sound system, electric blankets, lights. "These kinds of conveniences are part of the job of a good designer," says Spectre. "They might not have an impact on the visual effect of decoration, but they make things work behind the scenes." In Spectre's opinion, technology is true luxury.

After a decade of too many hours spent in traffic on the Long Island Expressway in the weekly commute to and from Southampton, Spectre sold the house. While renting a house in Connecticut, he bought land there and began an uphill struggle to build another country retreat. "I kept trying to get this house built, to get it off the ground, but it was like putting a square peg into a round hole," says Spectre. Eventually he came upon a house in the area that world-renowned architect Philip Johnson had designed in 1956. The first time he went to see it the real estate agent didn't show up, so he could only peek in the windows. Fortunately, there are a lot of them. "I thought, of all the houses I've looked at in the past two years, this is the right one — that is, if I really want a house that's this large and if I want to commit to a house," says Spectre. "I did and I did."

This appears to be the "big brother" of his former Southampton home; Spectre likes to say this is sheer coincidence. "I think Philip Johnson built a definitive twentieth-century home when he built my house. He knows it's my dream house. But I could live in other architects' houses; I enjoy a wide variety of styles." That an object have integrity — whether it is a house, a chair, or a sculpture — is the only real criterion for Spectre. "If I lived in a Corbusier house, I'd love it," he says. "But if I lived in a seventeenth-century house in Paris or a Regency house in London, I'd probably fall in love with it too. Well, maybe. I'm not positive about that because I've always lived in a very contemporary manner. The integrity of architecture fascinates me. I would find it difficult to live in a house with really bad architecture. I probably could do it, but I would continuously think about changing it and probably eventually would. I'd rather have little and less, than wrong."

Situated in a parklike setting, Deerfields, as the house is known, has a large thirty-two-foot-square, eighteen-foot-high central section — the living room — with wings to either side. One enters the structure through an outdoor pavilion area, set apart from the rest of the grounds by brick piers, overhead wood beams, and precise landscaping. The house is well integrated into its scenery, and a feeling of grandeur and dignity prevails without gratuitous ornament. Says Spectre: "Philip Johnson told me, 'This is not only my best house; this is my favorite house.' It was

something of a transitional house in his career, representing the moment when he began turning away from his strictly Miesian vocabulary and looking toward other precedents — classicism, the vernacular, Islamic, and other periods and styles."

However reverential Spectre is to the architecture, he has chosen not to treat it as a monument; the interiors respect the period but do not seek to re-create it. The decoration reveals his fully developed aesthetic. "I am a student of the twentieth century," says Spectre emphatically. "It's time that we realize what extraordinary technical and design achievements have been made in our century." His house pays homage to these marvels. It is not mired in the past. Perhaps most striking is Spectre's eclecticism. After many trips around the globe since his first experience abroad, Spectre is certainly worldly, able to tell you where to find the best Louis Quinze antiques in Paris, who makes the best bamboo furniture in Hong Kong, why he thinks Miami is an international city on the move. This savvy comes together in his house, where fine paintings, sculpture, antiques, and contemporary furniture find a serene harmony. "Communication, transportation, technology, have enhanced our eye," he says. "We have the advantage of being able to own and display a sixteenth-century Spanish table and a Marcel Breuer chair together."

Spectre refinished the oak panels of the living room, which had been bleached out by the sun. "Draperies are not a decorative extra but a necessity here," he says, so he replaced the shredded thirty-year-old floor-to-ceiling panels on the mainly glass sides of the room with fresh linen casement. As in a

Philip Johnson's "favorite house" —Deerfields, Jay Spectre's Connecticut country home.

Photograph by Peter Vitale.

Photographs by Peter Vitale.

conservatory, plants and trees grow wildly.

Spectre devised several seating groups, setting everything on the bias. He used large-scale pieces of furniture, including his signature overstuffed sofas in channeled brown leather. "The idea for channeling came out of the movies, out of thirties black-and-white film," remarks Spectre. "It has an interesting, somewhat sexy, silhouette. I've always been drawn to both tufted and channeled pieces, but the channeling seems to identify me and my point of view better than tufting. It adds sculptural value, plays games with the light, and is inviting."

Late Renaissance and Louis XIII pieces are among the antiques that Spectre mixes easily with other generously proportioned furnishings, primarily from the Orient. He chooses only pieces that are interesting sculpturally as well as usable. "I love the richness, the presence typical of the furniture of these periods," says Spectre. "It has a confidence, almost a swagger, that allows it to hold its own in what is a bold house." Eastern elements — Japanese screens, kilim pillows, the Persian rug against the brickwork floor, Chinese horseshoe-back chairs — lend a breath of luxury to what is a modernist room, amplifying its warmth rather than its austerity. "The Orient has always exerted a strong hold on me," says the designer. "I feel its mystery profoundly. I think it has to do with responding to forces beyond our knowledge."

ABOVE

A glimpse of Spectre's eclecticism: seventeenth-century Coromandel screen, contemporary leather sofa, and Tang ceramic figurine on late Renaissance Flemish table.

RIGHT

The dramatic living room at night with channeled sofa in the foreground and casual groupings of Giacometti pieces.

Photographs by Peter Vitale.

Sun-flooded view of
the living room facing the
paneled inner wall,
fireplace flanked by a
matched pair of
Giacometti console tables
made for Spectre
by the artist.

An intimate corner in the media room:
Spectre bronze bamboo chairs,
nineteenth-century Chinese armoire
housing a porcelain collection.

Spectre made only one big change to his house, the expansion of the kitchen to include a breakfast room. "We used the original brick left over from its construction," he says. "It was stacked in the garage." This room, warm and comfortable with its raised fireplace, terracotta tile floor, and wooden furniture, is where Spectre likes to host lunch and dinner parties. It is more intimate and relaxed than the dining room.

Spectre found his current Manhattan residence in a prewar building on upper Fifth Avenue while looking for one for a client. He believes in serendipity (as indeed one has to when looking for an apartment in New York City): "Like many things in life, this just happened to me. I guess that means I was ready for it." The eighth-floor apartment was in very bad shape — it had not been touched in thirty years — but was somehow just right. A total and complete renovation was the order of the day, starting from scratch with reconfiguration of the rooms, new wiring, plastering, lighting, and temperature-control systems. The placement of the master bedroom and the living room was reversed: Spectre chose to have his bedroom at the rear of the apartment away from the busy avenue where it would be quieter, and to use the Central Park view to advantage in the reception room.

The mood of this apartment is quite different from that of his former one, but the point of view has not changed, only matured. "Interiors are a mix of our life, of our soul, of who we are, where we've been, what we think," says Spectre. "My emphasis was on serenity, comfort, and quality. It doesn't have the fun or excitement of my other apartment, but that's not what I wanted here. I hate to

L E F T

The only addition to Deerfields: Spectre's sunny breakfast (and lunch and dinner) room.

say this, but it really is the apartment of a middle-aged man."

The decoration is pared down to the point where every object has its place and its purpose, where the palette is subdued and cohesive, and where space and vistas are maximized. "The apartment definitely has the ocean liner feel I love," says Spectre. "It is very carefully edited, which is after all what makes design or writing or painting good." The edited balance that emerges owes much to the intrinsic affinities shared by fine art, in Spectre's opinion. Last year he auctioned off most of his prized collection of Diego Giacometti furniture and sculptures at Sotheby's. "I don't want to be owned by my objects," he says forcefully. "I felt the time was right, so I did it. What I've kept is the memory of a twenty-year friendship with this artist. Editing, moving on, is a healthy process. It is what makes progress possible."

Like a painter defining the boundaries of a landscape, Spectre has framed the imposing view of Manhattan's West Side, magnifying it with a large picture window. The window seat, a channeled leather built-in chaise, and mirrored panels on the deep window reveals form a dramatic perch. Artfully covering one wall is mirror, an age-old space-enhancing trick. On the other walls handwoven raw silk from India is upholstered onto panels, a decorative system that lends the aura of a stage set to the interior. "When the walls are not up to snuff and the cost of replastering them is immense, it's often less trouble to panel," says Spectre's partner, Geoffrey Bradfield. "It also gives a rich feeling to a room — extremely soft and luxe." Spectre's choice of rustic bleached-oak pegged planks for the floor, rather than an elaborate

ABOVE

An elegant group: Germaine Derbecq painting, French Art Deco vases, and Giacometti cats on a rosewood demi-lune console.

RIGHT

The living room with Giacometti table, Arp sculpture, Herbin painting, Christofle vase, among other collectibles.

The channeled window seat
framing the dramatic view of
Central Park from Jay Spectre's
Manhattan apartment.

FAR RIGHT

The entrance gallery with
the Midavaine panels at right
and Eduardo Paolozzi sculpture
of Marilyn Monroe.

parquet, is deliberate. He wanted the room to be subdued and simple, an elegant backdrop for scene-stealing art and objects. "I tend toward textured neutrals today more than ever before," says Spectre of the mellow tones here. "I find them easier on the eye and easier to live with."

The theme of nature pervades the circular dining room and its adjoining entrance hall, which is hung with scenic painted panels by Louis Midavaine featuring white deer. Other references include the bronze birds by Giacometti, a gilded Tiffany dish that reminds Spectre of the sun, a Japanese screen of clouds and water, and the symbolic steel globe base of the round marble-topped table. When confronted with a high ceiling like this one, Spectre jumps at the chance to do something different, something glamorous. "Usually I try to lose ceilings, especially in small rooms," he says. Instead he commissioned an artist to create a handpainted and silver-leaf fantasy on canvas. Flickering candles exaggerate the metallic shimmer bounced off the ceiling, the shiny Barbara Hepworth bronze sculpture, and the art glass vases displayed in a curving wall vitrine.

The Art Deco aesthetic comes to the fore in the bedroom Spectre has created for himself — a taupe-toned cocoon of built-in furniture executed in white oak and replete with high-tech luxuries. "I believe in the personal environment as a shield, a buffer, a retreat from the realities one encounters outside the home," says Spectre. This is no exaggeration. The plush handmade carpet — the kind you can lose your toes in — is a dark ground for the wraparound oak desk and bedside table unit and the leather

The gleaming circular
dining room with
Ruhlmann dining chairs,
art glass vases, and
Barbara Hepworth bronze.

A painted bird flies across canvas
behind the Giacometti birds on
the dining room table.

Photographs by Peter Vitale.

upholstery of the bed and steamer chair, all Spectre designs. "The chair arm looks like a locomotive coming straight at you," he says. "That arm seems to represent very much for me one of the lines and attitudes of design of the first half of this century. It is a recurring part of my design vocabulary, the same way that artists like Arp and Moreau used the same symbols repeatedly."

A few of Spectre's favorite things surround him: He is especially fond of the small Edo screen because it depicts a treetop vista similar to the one revealed by the picture window in the living room. At the foot of the bed is a handpainted trunk modeled after a Japanese kimono chest from which, at the touch of a bedside button, rises a television. Says Spectre: "The technology, the buttons we push, are our servants of today."

The decoration of Spectre's city home is ten years old now, and he may be ready for something new — when he gets the courage. "After a lifetime of design and working with clients I have found what I first heard to be true: that our personal environments are mirrors of ourselves." Spectre's various dwellings are no exception. His first Manhattan apartment is very much a document of its time and the designer's developing point of view, and Spectre likes that. "I don't think interiors have to be timeless," he says. "I can show you work that hasn't been updated in twenty years that is still relevant though not necessarily of the instant. If it is exciting and represents its time honestly, that's good enough. I don't see any reason why a room has to be forever. It's more interesting when work documents a decade. The corrugated metal was an earlier me. I may be gearing up for a new reflection."

A corner of the bedroom showing a Spectre steamer chair, Raul Valdivieso marble torso and signed Art Deco table, Edo screen.

From There to Here

This is the story of a designer who takes chances. Jay Spectre is above all an innovator. "I have always been willing to take the risks entailed in being creative. The results may not please everyone. Some of my works may have been in style one year, out the next, but whatever they were, they were never safe or boring."

Spectre's unique vision, rooted in the twentieth century but not restricted by it, has been recognized by his clients, many of whom have come to him to design more than one of their homes. For one international couple, he has completed seven different residences. "My clients have almost always been self-made people, great achievers on their own, who are looking for a certain glamour, dignity, and quality in their surroundings," says Spectre. "They aren't always the most avant-garde, but they do want to live very much in the present." Spectre calls them the "silent celebrities," the invisible tycoons of today and tomorrow.

Like the soigné sets on which the Hollywood stars paraded, Spectre's interiors are stages for his clients' lives. And although he has discovered that real people don't look, act, or live like they do in the thirties movies he so enjoys, that doesn't stop Spectre from trying to re-create that glamour, that dizzy abandon, that Jazz Age spirit.

Jay Spectre finds working with art a privilege and a vital stimulus. His aim, similar to that of the first rank of professional interior decorators that sprang up in the twenties and thirties, is to unite fine art and applied arts in his designs. His distinctive synthesis relies on high-quality works of art from all periods and origins. "I am not afraid to mix," says Spectre. 'Somehow, an object takes on a wonderful look, an entirely different interpretation, in a contrasting environment. Look at the way antiquities displayed in a contemporary setting like a museum show up better than in their original context. A contemporary painting works the same way in a traditional decor."

The mystical Orient and this century's Moderne styles are the sources Spectre mines more than any others in his search for art, furniture, objects — and just plain inspiration. "I have a relationship to the thirties because I feel it was a very prolific period for art worldwide, whether in Japan or in France where fashion was at its zenith or in this country. It was a time of great contrasts, from the Great Depression to the extravagant living of the nouveau riche. More than anything, it was a time of great art achievements, from fashion to movies." Like the designers of this decade, Spectre draws exotic and primitive elements from such far-flung lands as the Far East and Africa.

Acquiring art for clients, collaborating with them on the foundations of a collection, can often be a part of the decorating job. When it is, Spectre enjoys the task immensely. "Most of the time my clients have reached a position in their lives where they can decide quickly and emphatically to acquire wonderful art, though they may only own it for a time," says Spectre, who believes we are custodians of these cultural artifacts, not owners.

2.
LIVING WITH ART

ABOVE

The Maillol bronze with her back to Central Park in New York City.

LEFT

The dramatic Fifth Avenue gallery, with Henry Moore sculpture, parquet de Versailles floor, and showcase lighting.

Spectre himself claims collecting doesn't run in his blood. "I share my personal tastes, my attitudes, with my clients," says Spectre, "but I am not a compulsive collector. I go about my personal acquisitions — I'm thinking of cuff links at the moment — in a much more casual way. One of my favorite pairs is a set of emerald ship's anchors I happened upon in New York. They are beautifully made; the backs are tiny gold life savers inscribed 'Hermès, Paris.' I took them to Hermès and they were intrigued because they had no record of the pattern, and I've heard they were made for the Duke of Windsor. Whatever their history, I just loved them on sight for their workmanship and whimsy. If I were a full-fledged collector, I can assure you I'd have a great deal more. I'm more interested in the special history or the provenance of a work of art or piece of furniture. The story fascinates me more than the physical reality." An interesting statement from a man who amassed enough of the iron sculpture and furniture of Diego Giacometti over their twenty-year friendship to have his own sale at Sotheby's in the spring of 1990. "I related to his work," he answers. "I really enjoyed living with it. To me, that's the beauty of owning something. I never bought for resale value."

With Spectre's enthusiasm for art and his belief in its power to alter the nature of a space, it is surprising that he doesn't attempt to control it more within the environments he so carefully constructs. "With rare exception I have never commissioned an artist to produce a piece of art specifically for a room," remarks Spectre. "When this has occurred, I am usually disappointed in it. Maybe the reason is that artists are best when they are spontaneous, unencumbered by other people's ideas or by a foreign environment that they are trying to conform to. The art object adapts to the environment and vice versa. It should be a marriage. I once asked Louise Nevelson to do a special piece of art for me for a client. She came to this grand apartment in her sable coat with a hammer in her pocket and two men to help her. We sat on the staircase and watched her create a piece of sculpture before our very eyes. I said to the clients, who didn't understand what they were witnessing, 'Something very important is happening here. This is an interesting moment. I want you to remember it.' The clients did not buy the sculpture that Nevelson built. They chose another piece of hers, but they didn't want the one that was created for them. Two or three years later I was having dinner with Louise at the Russian Tea Room and she said to me: 'You know, those people should have bought that sculpture. It is now on permanent exhibition at the Guggenheim.'"

Spectre's approach to setting off works of art varies. This depends on the personal tastes, lifestyle, and house of his clients, as well as the collection itself. One way is to construct spare, airy environments in which the decoration does not interfere with the enjoyment of the art. This is typified in his mid-1970s design of an apartment located in a modern, postwar building in New York City.

People say first impressions can make or break a relationship. "When I first met this client she wanted a Palm Beach apartment totally redecorated in the 'Palm Beach style.' I'd never been to Palm Beach and didn't know what it was, so I said, 'I'll do even better by you — I won't give you Palm Beach style.' The apartment was a success and we've gotten along swimmingly ever since." First

impressions can also decide the aesthetic fate of an interior, where entrance halls herald the mood of rooms beyond. Spectre transformed this New York apartment's entrance hall from a boring do-nothing, say-nothing space into an inspired gallery for sculptures and paintings. There is no furniture because there is no need for any. To impart an aura of hushed solemnity to the room, Spectre introduced these quick-change elements: an oversize parquet de Versailles floor, grand Louis XIV–style doors lacquered the color of cola, and dark rust mohair-velvet upholstery on the walls. He installed a custom version of showcase lighting, considered innovative at the time for residential use. Its polished bronze tubes wash the walls and art with warm, clear light and draw the eye away from the apartment's major shortcoming — low, concrete ceilings. A large Henry Moore sculpture of a reclining woman floats in the middle of the space, thanks to Spectre's imaginative design of a base and overhead lighting unit. "This was a good solution: It's a very professional treatment and doesn't bring in a piece of leggy furniture," he says.

Similarly, there is a restraint to the decoration of the narrow, L-shaped living room. "The art becomes especially important because the architecture is so poor," says Spectre. Focal points include the extraordinary 1919 Fernand Léger painting above the antique French stone mantel and the regal Buddha. To make the small apartment seem as spacious as possible, Spectre scrapped draperies and rugs in favor of the more pristine look of a bare floor and windows hung only with lacquered wood blinds. The overall emphasis is a sweeping horizontality. "I intentionally kept all the elements low, in order to invoke a sense of depth and space,"

says Spectre. "This created a deep focus, an illusion of distance — factors that are necessary when viewing paintings and sculpture." The sofa is upholstered in a pale diagonal-weave linen, the banquette, a great anchor for that corner, in dark mohair. Visual distractions are pared down to a few exotic accoutrements: a tortoiseshell and brushed-steel coffee table, a pair of eighteenth-century Portuguese benches.

Spectre turned the unusable cramped terrace adjoining the living room into a mise-en-scène starring a sublime Maillol bronze. He replaced what was an excessively ornate iron railing for the building (Spectre calls it "baroque funny business") with a sleek translucent divider of solar bronze glass. Dark mirror on the side walls and a brown ceiling complete the terrace's disappearing act, which is most dramatic in the evening. The only earthly reminders are the chevron-patterned brickwork and two potted ficus trees.

The designer took a different tack in displaying the art in the twenty-seven-room penthouse of Washington, D.C., clients. Uniting the vast interior is a bold and fresh riot of hues. "A traditional space plays on the emotions of the familiar, but it has to be energized with a contemporary sensibility," says Spectre. "One of the most exciting ways of doing this is through color. Really intense color comes almost full circle, turning into a neutral. This happens in fashion and painting too; think of Matisse or the Fauves."

Paintings by Gainsborough, Chagall, and Louis Valtat adorn the walls of the media room — no ordinary television hangout. It is as green as an emerald and equally jewellike in its intimacy. "The color is almost a controversial choice given the quality of the art there, but it is so effective," says Spectre.

The emerald media room.

Paintings by
Robert Motherwell and
Morris Lewis
together with a
gleaming Ernest Trova
statuette reflect
the brilliant tones
of the eighteenth-century
Heriz rug.

The vivid monochromatic decor focuses the
eye on the canvases and pre-Columbian
sculptures. Amplifying the green density is the
selection of material, a heavy mohair, which
Spectre upholstered on the built-in banquette,
armchairs, walls, ceiling, and roman shades.
To make the room feel even smaller, cozier,
he dropped the ceilings and installed lighting
coves tinted pale pink like "angel-skin coral."
Swiveling chairs enable you to turn away
from the conversation group and face the
entertainment center and bar. "I wanted to
create the ambience of a private railway
car or zeppelin," he says, "where one is
completely insulated from the realities of the
world."

The scale of the living room is especially
large, requiring fancy footwork on the part of
Spectre to ensure that its occupants not feel
overwhelmed by its grandeur. To minimize
the contrast between this room's sixteen-foot
ceilings and the more modest height of the
adjoining foyer, Spectre installed a transom
of fragmented mirror for a trompe l'oeil effect.
A pair of freestanding Corinthian stone
columns flanking the doorway offer a whimsical allusion to a classical facade. These
architectural details also create a compelling
backdrop for the art.

The departure point for the decorating is
clearly the eighteenth-century Heriz rug, its
brilliant tones picking up those in the other
furnishings as well as in the paintings. Silk-
wrapped walls and deep upholstered
furniture in a thick textured cotton, all off-
white, are comfortable counterpoints to the
opulent colors and surfaces of such pieces
as the Steinway piano, which Spectre had
refinished to resemble Macassar ebony;
the red Robert Motherwell canvas; and the
gleaming Ernest Trova statuette. "I made the

ceiling navy blue just like one in an old movie house because it was so far away," says Spectre. Oriental and Persian accessories accentuate the intentionally international mix of objects, somehow just right for the nation's capital city. Says Spectre of the larger-than-life quality in this room: "The American genius has always been about finding the satisfaction in daily life. In Europe the burden of history sometimes stifles creative energy, preventing innovation and inhibiting spontaneity. This apartment possesses the best of traditional design infused with the vigor, breadth, and boldness of a distinctly American perspective."

In a charming prewar building on Manhattan's fashionable Sutton Place is an apartment Spectre revamped to be, he feels, "a retreat from the harshness of the city, an oasis in the world's most exciting jungle." The composition revolves around the art and the skyline, the decorative radiance around his signature use of burnished surfaces. "Here I've deliberately kept the patterns subtle, as I didn't want them to compete with the art," says Spectre. "My aim was a peaceful ambience."

Spectre composed a simple setting in the living room with bleached-wood floors, smooth eggshell walls, and pale curtain panels. He used casual fabrics — a pale Fortuny print and an off-white textured chevron cotton — and arranged the furnishings in a conventional manner. Elements of luxury and glamour punctuate, rather than overload, the room. The ceiling, covered in gold-leafed canvas, casts a moody glow; it is opulent, but without the choking formality of some gilding.

Beneath this burnished awning Spectre has reworked antiques for contemporary effect.

A close-up view of the Sutton Place living room, with two Giacometti lamps on the mantelpiece flanking *Samurai 9* by Robert Motherwell.

He zipped up a pair of nineteenth-century French carved armchairs by upholstering them in black horsehair with seat backs in contrasting black-and-white horse weave. "I love the texture of horse hair," says Spectre, who imports it from Paris. "It's rich and practically indestructible, and it transcends periods, looking good on everything from Victorian to contemporary furniture." He rewired Giacometti lamps with telephone cords and placed them as garniture on the neoclassical stone mantel. "Glamour is often about surprises," says Spectre. "Sometimes the out-of-context use of a particular material makes everything more interesting. The same goes for fashion. I love satin and tweed together." Eclectic or not, the room's subtle quality and simplicity flatter the art, which seems integrated into the decoration rather than ostentatiously on display.

Departing from the neutral palette of the living room, Spectre chose tartan-strong colors rendered in slick finishes for his version of a masculine library, a cozy retreat where pipe-smoking or curling up with a good book seems almost encouraged by the decor. He retained the period plaster moldings and painted the walls a dark green enamel. This lacquered look is a sympathetic backdrop for the numerous Oriental objects and furnishings placed here and there.

Spectre chose red as a counterpoint. It is peppered throughout the room: in the focal-point still life by Léger, on the cognac leather sofa (quilted diagonally like a Chanel bag for extra detail), in the antique Persian carpet, and on the inside of the bar cabinet. The bar's outside doors are disguised in leather dummy book bindings, mirroring the bookcase at the other end of the sofa. "The faux-library idea is not a new idea by any

A corner of the library showing bar doors lined with japanned lacquer screens contrasting with dark green enameled walls and the focal Léger still life.

Two views of a Sutton Place library in Manhattan.

means," says Spectre. "It was used a lot in the late seventeenth century in Italy and France. Trompe l'oeil is fun in the right spot, if it amuses and fools."

The master bedroom is one of the most beautiful rooms Spectre believes he has ever designed. It is awash with the apricot-peach-pear tones of the handpainted silk that wraps the walls, frames the windows, and covers the bed. Texture is abundant, yet there is a plainness that is easy on the eye. Spectre placed elegant draperies within the outer reveals, surrounding the picture windows. So that his clients could enjoy the enclosed view together, he designed a double-width daybed within the window alcove. Technology is not forgotten, only well disguised in a pilaster sheathed in fabric. This automated media unit opens by remote control. By Spectre's own standards this room is a success. His measure? When an interior really complements its owners.

Spectre conveyed the immediacy of much of this century's art in a sprawling 1940s Dallas house that he renovated with an architect for a young couple and their two sons. The decoration is well suited to Texas in its modernity and its bold color, space, comfort. It is also especially appropriate for the owners' collection of contemporary art, where an easy interaction prevails. This is very clear in the entrance hall, a thirty-foot gallery that leads from the front door into the family room. To make the rectilinear space more dynamic and architecturally interesting, Spectre installed a floor, faux marble with ebony-and-white geometric shapes, a kind of semiotic reference to modernism. Its whimsy keeps the entry from being overwrought and too formal.

The attitude of the furnishings and art is fun and lighthearted too. A grouping of sculptures is set beside a terracotta pot of bulbs on a Michael Graves console, and a 1984 Frank Stella print swirls above it. One even feels an urge to hang the car keys from one of the hooks in Jim Dine's 1962 *Colorful Hammer Rack*, which hangs opposite.

34

Looking down the faux marble entrance hall hung with a 1984 Frank Stella and Jim Dine's 1962 *Colorful Hammer Rack*.

An adjoining gallery was one of the by-products of the house's remodeling. "We found we had an extra room that you had to walk through to get to the new living room," says Spectre, who turned it into an anteroom for displaying art. The walls are intentionally clear for pictures, the space left open for sculpture. The only piece of furniture is a round banquette in the center of the room so the occupants can sit and enjoy the art from any angle.

In the gallery, paintings by Sam Gummelt, Tom Holland, Al Held.

Perhaps the most dramatic space is the living room, where Spectre created a look of lush simplicity. "The couple was not interested in overdecorating," says Spectre. He pared down the room's shell, editing moldings right out of the picture, then painting the walls to resemble limestone blocks. Spectre's love of the all-white Art Deco interiors he saw in the old Hollywood movies inspired the white palette, achieved with a handwoven braided carpet and matching thickly textured chevron fabric on oversize sofas and steamer chairs. This setting is punctuated by opulent eye-catchers: a shapely gilded Regency mirror, a 1960 Kenneth Noland bull's-eye canvas, an eighteenth-century Italian commode. The tour de force is the window treatment. Spectre framed French doors running along the terrace with shimmering cobalt silk curtains edged with gold thread, as though they were royal ball gowns. "I wanted the overall look to be cool because it gets so hot there," says Spectre. "The curtains could have been any cool color, just as easily green as blue, and the effect would have been very much the same. It just so happens that the owners prefer blue."

Classic patterns and shapes from the Jazz Age triggered Spectre's decoration of the dining room. He revived a Sonia Delaunay design from the twenties on handpainted silk, padding the walls and draping the entryway with it. The fabric's pale aqua tone and painterly treatment lend an understated romance to the room. Spectre suggested updating Queen Anne—style chairs with new upholstery. The client needlepointed the seat covers in different, but coordinating, geometric designs. Echoing these Cubist-derived patterns is the staircase carpet, a

38

A deceptively simple white living room. Kenneth Noland bull's-eye canvas hangs between two romantically draped windows.

The romantic,
eminently sociable
dining room adorned
with a dramatic
Helen Frankenthaler
painting.

Spectre design, visible in the hall beyond. Other affinities are perhaps less intentional: The large 1968 painting by Helen Frankenthaler pushes the theme of abstraction even further with its elusive message.

A family room becomes a garden room when Spectre opens it up with unadorned floor-to-ceiling glass to the lush grounds outdoors. This is accentuated by mint-green mohair banquettes and a green-and-white floral Irish carpet. The furnishings are intentionally spare so that the atmosphere will be airy and light. Spectre kept the walls basic, painting them no-nonsense off-white, and designed a simple chimney breast of white oak, which holds a Larry Rivers portrait of the wife. "The house is livable, even for the children," he says. "It's clean and uncluttered, sophisticated but still relaxed.

"An art collection of exceptional quality demands an environment of similar quality," says Spectre. "In this way the art and the decoration show each other off to advantage, with the overall visual effect that much stronger." Spectre achieved this aesthetic orchestration in a Toronto apartment. The civic-minded owners are true art lovers who own many important Impressionist and Post-Impressionist paintings. Spectre's challenge here was to display the pictures in a complimentary setting and satisfy the demands of comfortable day-to-day living.

Spectre achieved this goal by composing an unobtrusive backdrop in the rooms. In the entrance hall and living room, he paneled the walls in a neutral-toned raw silk; in the dining room, he used mirror and lightly stained oak. The floors throughout are the same pale oak, "nothing fancy at all," says Spectre. This simple treatment heightens the luxury and

profusion of rich hues in the paintings. Spectre
further enforced this almost casual attitude in
the living room with quilted Fortuny cotton in
cushions on chairs and on overstuffed sofas.
"We tried hard to make the room inviting,"
says Spectre. "When you are decorating
with art, you don't want people to feel
intimidated because of the museum-quality
works on display."

The clients love to entertain, and so does
Spectre. The dining room reflects their festive
attitude, its decoration flexible enough to
accommodate the most formal of five-course
meals as well as a casual buffet. To suit the
overscale octagonal table, Spectre chose
ample Queen Anne–style armchairs to
surround it. "Their colorful cotton upholstery is
a Matisse-like print that is whimsical and fun,
not overly grand," says Bradfield. Spectre
also integrated furnishings and art in his
design of the room's rug. It features a tassel-
motif border, which Spectre derived from
the golden ornamentation of the owners'
collection of Fabergé eggs.

Toronto can be cold and gray, so Spectre
made the master bedroom warm and sunny.
"The colors were picked right out of the two
Marie Laurencin paintings," says Bradfield.
Unlike the other rooms in the apartment,
this one is blue and yellow. "The palette
is cohesive because the art is cohesive,"
explains Spectre. "These colors, prevalent
in the period's art, make it look good."

It is hard to imagine ever wanting to leave
the bedroom, with its warm cocoon of
bundled surfaces. The headboard, mattress,
and base are upholstered in a matching
quilted floral, as are the chaise longue and
an armchair. "A bedroom's function never
changes," says Spectre. "There's only so

42

much you can do when it comes to the basic design, so we focus on decorating with different finishes, surfaces, textures." More abstract than the primary floral are the squiggles of the handpainted canvas applied to the walls and the harlequin pattern of the plush carpet.

This room may seem rather traditional for such an "up-to-the-minute" designer. Spectre doesn't care. "Decorating is not an exact science," he says. "The days of a designer who offers an all-purpose 'look' tucked under his arm are over. Today it is crucial to spend time with people, to absorb the spirit of their thinking and their locale in order to give them what they've dreamed of having but may not have known how to articulate. This is right for these people.

"I try to have an open mind when it comes to decorating and art," adds Spectre. "To be rigid is inhibiting — and it makes the job more difficult. I like to shop, design, decorate with a very open mind. That's sometimes hard for my clients, but it's very much a part of my personality and really the only way I like to approach decorating."

Spectre is someone who doesn't like to be typecast, and the diversity of his rooms shows it. "I am always looking for the unusual, for the innovative. I'll never get over the desire for an artistic achievement. I'm thrilled when something really comes together and works. I have a client in Washington who says, 'Jay, you love your own work.' You know, she's right. Most of the time."

3. ULTRA URBAN

A belief in total design shapes Spectre's sleek handling of urban interiors. "What I loved from the era of the great ocean liners, the twenties and thirties, was how everything down to the last button and knob, from the wineglasses to the coolers to the fabrics at the windows, was brought together into one elegant statement." This marriage of luxury and economy of design suits Spectre to a tee, and his urban interiors reveal his talents at their best. He likes the challenge of achieving optimum function and versatility.

"So much of the twentieth century lies behind us now," says Spectre. "It's time we reappraised it. What we come away with is a new appreciation of the breakdown between formal and informal ways of living, which has influenced the way we eat, dress, sleep, work, relax, even our manners. Think about the impact these changes have on a room."

There are other factors besides an urban setting that determine the decoration of a home, primarily the wishes of the client. For example, the first apartment Spectre designed in New York was for a couple who wanted a country look in the city, at a time when French country was becoming very popular. The design met the clients' requirement, but Spectre gave it his particular twist, combining it with city sophistication and cutting-edge technology. The best elements of French country were picked up and spun around, recombined with his point of view. "Environment is a state of mind as much as anything else and depends a great deal on the participants," says Spectre. "I like to create an attitude."

Spectre never did a country look in the city again. "If anything, our urban interiors have

had more of an impact on the way we decorate country homes," says Bradfield. Spectre was drawn instead to the seemingly limitless possibilities of high-tech. One of his most avant-garde projects is the Manhattan apartment he designed for Clarence House president Robin Roberts in the early 1970s. The apartment remains exactly the same nearly two decades later. Today it is really a period interior, capturing, as it does, Spectre's futuristic vision of that moment. "I thought it was the responsibility of the interior designer to bring something to the table, to take the client further than he originally wanted to go," explains Spectre. "Actually that's not the responsibility of the interior designer. It's just my responsibility."

Here is the much-touted first "media room," a phrase coined by Spectre with journalist Joan Kron, to describe the viewing lounge he created in the living room. The era of home videos — the rise of the Betamax — had just dawned. Spectre saw it happen and brought the picture palace into our houses. His design of a brushed-steel projection cabinet lined with crocodile was shocking. Why would anyone put these two disparate materials together? Spectre loved the juxtaposition of textures and finishes, as well as the controversy. "I think video changed decoration, in the same way that television changed our lifestyle," says Spectre. "To me, technology goes hand in hand with glamour. I love the idea of pushing a button and having draperies move or the lights go on all over the house or the lights dim in another room." Spectre's more recently completed interiors reveal his fondness for the creature comforts brought about by new technology. "We're designing an interior now where the lighting

NEAR RIGHT

The intergalactic entryway with Botero drawing.

FAR RIGHT

A vintage brushed-steel projection cabinet in the media room, circa 1968.

and the sound are done by computer," he says. "If I had my way, those are the changes I would make in my house and in my apartment. I would do them before aesthetic changes. I think that's very much the way to live today."

Spectre encased the walls of the entrance hall in brushed steel. For a warm counter-point, he stained the oak floor dark espresso brown and painted the ceiling a high-gloss aubergine purple. Walking into the corridor is like walking into the belly of a spaceship, but not quite, because of the reminders of the human touch: the Venetian parquet of the floor, a large Botero drawing, a primitive mask. This was no afterthought on Spectre's part. Fantasy walls and ceilings need the grounding of handwrought art.

Hunter-green mohair walls and ceilings in the living room set off the bright red and dramatic form of the Ben Johnson painting.

Revolutionary
mirrored walls reflect
eighteenth-century
Portuguese chairs
in this late-sixties
dining room.

48

The Lucite headboard in the bedroom exemplifies Spectre's evolving use of unconventional materials.

Spectre experimented with other materials too, always tempering the hard-edged with the human dimension. In the living room, he upholstered the walls and ceiling in hunter-green mohair. Shots of intense color — orange leather on the wraparound sofa, blood-red velvet on the velvet club chair — were inspired by the Ben Johnson painting. Other than the ebullient use of color, the decoration is fairly stripped down. Primitive stools from Africa and Polynesia are handcrafted accents to the dominant Louise Nevelson wall piece and shiny bronze figure by Ernest Trova. In the dining room, Spectre turned to mirror for the walls, exploiting this material as a sparkling backdrop for entertaining. It was applied precut in a chevron pattern, and in Spectre's hands, it is as precious and glamorous as gold or silver.

The master bedroom is more Spartan. There is no real furniture to speak of, none of the accoutrements of comfort that we all expect in our most private room. Spectre sheathed the whole space, top, sides, and bottom, in industrial gray carpeting for a snug sense of enclosure. In the center of the room he positioned a freestanding bed with a brushed-steel base and orange leather fitted mattress treatment, and updated the notion of a headboard with his Lucite design. It stretches from the floor to the ceiling, lending the suggestion of structure to the rectangular room without partitioning it. The headboard's connected shelf unit holds a primitive mask.

"When I stopped worrying about good taste, my ideas began to flow," says Spectre. "Elsie de Wolfe said something that was particularly American and on-target: 'Vulgarity is a very important ingredient in life. A little bad taste is like a nice splash of paprika.'"

Some people who saw Roberts's apartment walked away greatly disturbed by the decoration. A couple of the owner's friends stopped speaking to him and never did again. "They didn't understand it," says an amused Spectre. "Like many things that are new, it represented a challenge and a threat. The way contemporary art challenges you and ultimately stimulates you."

"Interior design should always deal with interpreting the times we live in," says Spectre. "A room can be a visual summing up, even if that design is an invention of the self, a past, a future, a life." Spectre's personal affection for drama, theatricality, innovation often appear in his decorating. "I've given my clients glamour when it was appropriate and applicable to the personality involved," he says. "I don't think it's what material you use but how you use it. The element of surprise is essential."

Spectre played with this idea of glamour in a much more traditional interior, an eleven-room Manhattan duplex he decorated in the early 1970s for a Beverly Hills couple. Architect Stanford White had designed the landmark building on Fifth Avenue, and the apartment still retained a great many of the original elements, including an iron stair railing, a marble entrance-hall floor, and the configuration of the rooms. Spectre, sensibly enough, left them all intact. "If you respect the innate style of places and objects, you can hardly go wrong," he says. What he brought to the apartment was a style and an attitude that both suited the client and maintained the integrity and elegance of the magnificent location and architecture.

To Spectre, the duplex captured the essence of a jet-set lifestyle. At the time he

50

LEFT

A view of the
central staircase
anchored by a
Dubuffet sculpture.

RIGHT

A perfect
period room,
Spectre's
early-seventies
media room.

said, "I challenge you to place this room geographically. Isn't this a sort of ultimate metropolitan space?" Indeed, the atmosphere evokes the black-and-white films from the heyday of Hollywood, with its sweeping staircase, majestic spaces, formal entertaining areas. It conveys unrepentant luxury.

There is a distinctly contemporary aspect to each room, from the olive-green carpet running up the central staircase to the red chevron-cut glass walls of the dining room with its neoclassical moldings. "This was very new at the time," says Spectre of the red mirror. He envisioned this room as an updated version of the Brighton Pavilion, with its blue-and-white Chinese porcelains, its crystal and glass, its dark wood floor. "It has a Regency flavor with a late-twentieth-century attitude."

Spectre enlivened the center hall with a metal grille ceiling that showered the windowless space with filtered light. The new mesh ceiling makes the hall a virtual open-air pavilion. "I wanted to place the room fully in the current moment," says Spectre. "It wasn't a question of taking away from the architecture. Would I do it today? I doubt it." It did serve a purpose, however, bringing the colors and textures of the living room, dining room, and library together. Spectre chose gold foil for the walls to further accentuate the magical shimmer. Together, the ceiling and walls become an effective backdrop for sculptures and objects, including a nineteenth-century red lacquer table from the Orient, as well as for its bicoastal owners.

The designer isn't always presented with such gracious apartments. Spectre savors the challenge of difficult small spaces, the chance to stretch his creative resources. So much the better if an apartment is just a shoe box or

51

a series of little rooms like a rabbit warren. Zeppelins, automobiles, and railroad cars are his inspiration for creating surprising solutions that please both client and designer. Sometimes the intimate scale of a smaller room can be very comforting. "With a small space we always attempt expansion," says Bradfield. "The way we do that is by giving it cohesion. Usually you will find that one color is followed throughout to avoid a dramatic transition between rooms."

For a young man in his early twenties and his frisky pet labrador, Spectre renovated a cramped penthouse (its saving grace is a generous terrace for romping on) into a fun, functional bachelor's flat. The client, who had studied at Cambridge University in England, is somewhat of a traditionalist, so he did not want the interior to be too radical. Spectre obliged by decorating with an eye to the past, choosing only classics for this very current, very contemporary expression.

Spectre devised the layout of the apartment so that the warmth and appeal of the fireplace could be enjoyed from its adjoining rooms, the dining room/entrance hall, the bedroom, and the living room. Endowing the interconnected space with a sense of architecture was not an easy feat: Spectre added the large-scale zigzag of the chevron parquet on the floor and the steppe detailing of the ceiling. Says Spectre, "Usually we would have installed cove lighting to conceal the beams and still maintain the height, but the client really likes the look of beams. We incorporated them into the ceiling for a very architectural look."

From chevron parquet to the steppe detailing on the ceiling, the gleaming wood throughout this interconnected space gives the feeling of an elegant cigar box.

Looking through the cozy library/sitting room area toward the living room.

From the dining table that rolls on casters into a niche when not in use to the pocket doors of the bedroom, space is maximized. Spectre does not like waste of any kind, and no one could afford to waste space here. The fireside grouping is the merest suggestion of a library, with its tall built-in bookcases and cushy leather armchairs. Signed victory game footballs from the Cleveland Browns (the team owner is the client's father) are set on the mantel, a masculine choice with its brass-studded detailing. Other evidence of his passion for the sport — framed photographs, personal mementos — is arranged on the nearby bedroom wall, and propped up in corners are the guitars the client, an amateur musician, collects.

Signed footballs grouped casually on a sophisticated marble mantel.

The bedroom shares the intimacy of the fireplace through two pocket doors.

The living room is dominated by a massive 1633 oil portrait of a Florentine senator. The brilliant reds of the painted gown eliminate the need for a lot of color elsewhere. Spectre pared the room down to a few essentials, focusing on an appealing range of textures and finishes, rather than more color, to arouse interest. He encased the wall of mirrors in wild-oak paneling. "The client likes this traditional treatment," explains Bradfield. An eighteenth-century elmwood credenza with bronze trappings is flanked by a pair of forties chairs (the only pieces of furniture the client brought with him), which Spectre jazzed up with black horsehide. That great thirties icon, the *Normandie* ocean liner, contributed not only the document pattern for the silk of the pillows but also the nickel-and-alabaster sconces.

LEFT

A classic Spectre
grouping:
seventeenth-century
Italian oil painting,
signature channeled
armchairs,
and Giacometti
coffee table.

RIGHT

The living room
captured in the
mirrored wall.
Two black lacquer
Hibachi vases
punctuate
the space.

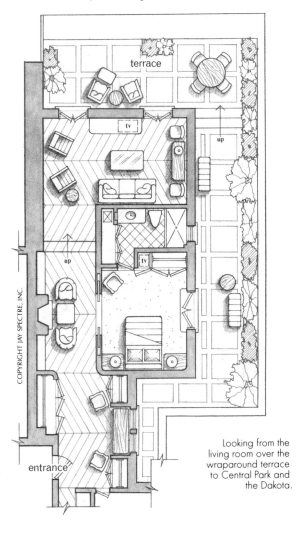

A blueprint showing the wraparound terrace.

terrace

tv

up

up

tv

entrance

Looking from the
living room over the
wraparound terrace
to Central Park and
the Dakota.

The
terrace plan
for the Manhattan
penthouse.

In another Manhattan apartment, this one a minimal 1920s shoe box, Spectre developed a subtle interplay of living spaces — connected yet distinct — for the pied-à-terre of an international couple. Spectre treated the main room and the master bedroom as a suite of rooms, one flowing into the other, as he did the two different areas in the main room. Each is quietly distinguished within the cohesive decorating scheme. A diagonal white-oak floor and mirrored side walls lend formality to the dining area. Spectre broke the rear wall into three panels positioned at small angles to each other for a more purposeful niche. Reflective vitrines cut within this triad of panels — a virtual stage set for dining — hold Kangxi-period porcelains and famille verte vases. A 1936 Picasso lingers against the mirrored wall.

An eight-inch platform calls for a single step up to the sitting area and the open bedroom, which Spectre carpeted continuously in the same textured wool. "The platform was built so you would better appreciate the view," says Spectre. "This way you have a slightly higher vantage point." A lone picture window reveals the jagged skyline of Central Park South and the bushy green treetops. To bring as much as possible of this real-life canvas inside, mirrors were used on the window reveals, on the partial back wall of the sitting area, and on the wall opposite the bedroom, which is mostly covered with a lush Japanese screen. Throughout the apartment, the walls are upholstered in raw silk and the coloration is neutral, in muted copper tones, to create a "templelike calm," as Bradfield describes it, and a soft setting for art. Two small bronze figures by Archipenko and Degas are lit by the sunlight pouring in through the

LEFT

Dual function entry/dining area with 1936 Picasso still life.

ABOVE

A view of Central Park South from the slightly raised sitting room attended by a Degas sculpture.

window, and two Tamayo paintings frame the entry to the bedroom. Centered on the wall within it, a Picasso portrait stares out into the main room.

The owners rarely entertain at their Manhattan residence. For the occasional times when they do, pocket doors were devised to seal off the bedroom from peering eyes. The doors are enlivened with subtle metallic checks, a Cubist-inspired detail popular in the Moderne era. The designer has worked it so that the sitting area is not only a living room for the apartment but a conversation nook for the bedroom. A pair of club chairs provide a decorative transition between the adjoining rooms: They are pulled opposite the banquette, yet their suede upholstery is the same as that which covers the nearby bed.

Another example of vintage Spectre inventiveness is the bed treatment. "We created an allusion to a traditional canopy," says Spectre, who had squares of padded suede applied to the wall and ceiling for an enclosing coziness and hint of structure.

"We focused on creating a still life of space, a long, angular pool of light and shade," he says of his decorating philosophy here. This is perhaps most evident in the study, where a horsehide sofa, Louise Nevelson wall sculpture, and shiny desk — all in black — form sharp silhouettes against the soft silk-hung wall. Spectre chose a Mies van der Rohe chair in bright blue leather for a needed jolt of color and fun, the same reason he piled dazzling blue pillows on the main room's banquette.

62

A serene
Picasso portrait
looks over the suede
canopied bed.

63

Spectre is well versed in the classic styles of decoration, although he has seldom designed period rooms, choosing instead to mix the best of each era for a look that best suits the client and the space. An exception is the renovation of the lobby of his 1935 Fifth Avenue apartment building, a task he took on at the request of the tenants' committee. The goal was an entry that complemented the building: its architecture, its period, its location. Spectre decided to interpret this aim in a strict fashion, partly because of his love for Art Deco, the building's style. Now it has all the old-time sophistication of an Irving Berlin or a Cole Porter song. He embellished the room's sense of architecture by adding trompe l'oeil columns to frame the bronze elevator doors, and furnished it with period pieces. The existing marble floor dictated a palette of gunmetals and platinums, that cinematic black and white again. Particularly spectacular are the period French light fixtures. "It was a historical interpretation," says Spectre. "We just did it this way because the space commanded it."

The Art Deco lobby at 955 Fifth Avenue.

Spectre revamped an Upper East Side Manhattan townhouse for a professional man who required office space on the first floor and gracious living on the upper four stories. Starting at the top, Spectre reclaimed space from the roof (it is virtually impossible nowadays to get permission to do this from the landmarks commission) for a conservatory room. The atmosphere is relaxed for easy lounging and entertaining. Director's chairs — as much a staple of country porch decorating as a fixture of film sets — capture the room's mood, part open-air pavilion, part media room. From the ceiling hangs a projector for home movie watching and nightclub-style Ruhlmann lamps.

67

A breath of the country in the city: the conservatory capping a Manhattan townhouse.

"We wanted to give him unusual spaces for living," says Spectre, who reconfigured the dining room, kitchen, and living room. The corner of the kitchen jutted out into the passage between the dining and living areas: Spectre had the wall rounded off and hung a Japanese screen there. "It softened the approach to the living room," he explains.

The goal for the living room was a "traditional elegance, at once old and new," according to its designer. A cornerstone of the new room is a dramatic Art Deco—inspired chimney breast of paradisio marble with corners of brushed steel. A Fortuny print echoes the soft coloration of the marble and the Japanese screen. "The pattern is from a fourteenth-century Venetian document, and it's as contemporary as tomorrow," says Spectre.

Spectre continued the lush mix of materials in the adjoining dining room, where Ruhlmann chairs in a Ruhlmann fabric are paired with a signed period table of burl walnut. The tablescape is simple, yet composed of objects of great quality. "There's a constant contrast of texture — marble, steel, thick raw silk on the walls, chinoiserie tables — without the overstuffed quality of some apartments," says Bradfield.

A B O V E

Detail of marble mantel showing art glass vase.

L E F T

A quintessentially warm and sophisticated living room, defined by a glorious marble chimney breast and Japanese screen.

70

A corner of the
living room
with Fortuny
venetian print
window
treatment.

The sculpture *Stairway to the Void* guards the sensuous profile of the Ruhlmann dining table and chairs.

Embodied in the small Fifth Avenue apartment of Carl Levine, senior vice president of Bloomingdale's, is Spectre's most current statement, a swank bachelor pad in the true Hollywood sense. "It evokes the atmosphere of a Jack Warner type of movie," says Spectre. "Very much a man's apartment." Spectre and the client shopped together for over a year in search of just the right place. They finally settled on an apartment that had not been touched since the 1940s. "Of all the spaces we looked at, this one needed the most work," says Spectre. There was simply nothing to be salvaged, a good thing in one respect. It allowed Spectre to create something totally new, totally unique, and very much his point of view. "It's definitely 1990s, although there are echoes of many other eras, especially the twenties," says Spectre.

72

The dramatic entry hall paneled in bird's-eye maple.

A cosmopolitan Manhattan entrance hall.

What is new is the absolute refinement, the sumptuous simplicity. Spectre had virtual free reign to create this expression: The client, very much a believer in the design vernacular of the firm, had few specific requirements for his new home. Spectre was to create a hand-tailored, aesthetically pleasing apartment for a tasteful, fastidious individual with a definite sense of style. "The apartment is very much about me," says Levine. "It has great strength and I am usually identified as having a very strong personality."

"The elements all have some derivation, but they've become much more purified and pristine," explains Bradfield. "The lines of the apartment may remind you of Art Deco lines, but they're not. That's what's very exciting about it."

Spectre reconfigured the apartment so that the library, living room, and entrance hall would now form classical spaces. "We added a tremendous amount of architecture," he says. "We also had to conceal a lot of existing beams which had no poetry. They were just rigid — typical of a 1940s building." Spectre introduced wonderful chamfers at the ceiling, which form zigzag walls in the corners. Rather than long, narrow, funneled rooms, the architecture staggers back and forth, giving the interior a rhythm and dimension that wouldn't exist ordinarily.

Spectre paneled the walls in bird's-eye maple stained a rich cognac color, and, where there is no paneling, he upholstered it in fabric from his collection for a deliberate touch of softness. The apartment's main axis, composed of an entry area, open hall, and vestibule, is defined spatially with sharp racing-stripe lines of black lacquer set within the wood and a graphic faux travertine-and-black-granite floor.

Few bachelors dine formally alone, so Spectre scrapped the idea of a full-blown dining room. In its place he designed a sitting area, a banquette with an upholstered leather back on the wall and French Art Deco chairs in the Chinese style, from which a media unit concealed in the wall opposite can be enjoyed. When entertaining is the order of the day, a convertible-size dining table can be rolled out from its built-in hiding place beneath the adjacent window ledge. Distinguishing the area from the open wall is the tête-de-nègre finish and slightly sunken level of the floor.

Across the hall is the living room, where Spectre has played with eurythmic lines and geometry for a masculine-looking decoration. The interplay of shapes in the Ruhlmann-inspired rug by Spectre, the oil painting by Frank Faulkner installed against one wall, and the checkered brushed-steel lamp catch and stimulate the eye. Many of the furnishings are of impeccable quality: a signed Rousseau table of shagreen and palmwood, a pair of Ruhlmann chairs in taupe leather, vitrines housing a collection of pre-Columbian art.

Spectre brings an exuberance to decorating projects like this that can easily incorporate the dynamic symbols of the past, still resonant with energy and ready to be appropriated by a new generation. Jay Spectre's silent celebrities have their own style to contribute to the ongoing tradition of American glamour.

Spectre's bachelor dining room is a study in controlled energy.

The classic
Stanford White
front hall/gallery
framing a bronze
wing sculpture by
Christian Renonciat.

4.

MANSIONS AND PARKS

While his clients' tastes, desires, and demands make each decorating job different, some radically so, Jay Spectre's point of view is constant. "I knew a long time ago that my point of view would always be somewhat contemporary, that it would be eclectic, that it would probably have many different elements from all over the world," says Spectre. His approach is discernible even in the more traditional settings of grand houses. In the same way that the sophisticated flavor of Manhattan calls for a heightened urbane mood in a pied-à-terre there, a Connecticut manor house dictates an altogether different temperament. "Local products and influences affect my design vocabulary, no doubt about it," says Spectre. "An example is a house we did in Okinawa, Japan, where we were inspired by the textiles, colors, and lacquer-work the area is known for." The same holds true for Colorado or Southern California.

Landmark-quality architecture formed the decoration of a San Francisco house. Spectre loves the mystical quality of light in this charming bay city, where townhouses are sandwiched together up the sides of its famously steep streets. One of these, in the Georgian tradition, was designed by the neoclassical architect Stanford White and finished posthumously in 1910. "This is a house that had all the character in the world," says Spectre. "The challenge here was to fulfill the needs of the clients while preserving the integrity of the architecture."

The three-story structure is generously proportioned, revolving around a central staircase. Dark mahogany paneling, Tudor-style plasterwork on the ceiling, and the dramatic scale are expansively American in spirit. Spectre decided to leave well enough alone on the room-size second-floor landing, approaching the design from a furnishings standpoint.

"I've always had a healthy respect for the past," says Spectre. "I am fascinated with the history of architecture and furniture, although I'm not inclined to repeat it." In this interior Spectre worked within the confines of history, selecting objects and pieces of furniture from ancient Asia, the seventeenth century, and the twenties and thirties. This eclecticism brings a distinctly exotic dimension to the interiors, appropriate for a city that is a gateway to the Far East. One of the new furnishings is a pale carpet runner for the stairs, which functions as a counterpoint to the heaviness of all the polished wood; its rich border was derived from the graphic motifs of an antique Persian rug in the entrance hall below. Set within this gallery space like jewels are several prized pieces collected by the couple and Spectre on their many shopping trips together: a red tortoiseshell table inlaid with ebony and ivory, a fourteenth-century Ming fresco at the top of the stairs, a patinated bronze wing sculpture by Christian Renonciat.

Spectre's delicate handling of draperies is surprising to those accustomed to his more austere treatments. Here, he has delved back into history for their design, reviving a Louis XIII style: three-quarter-length shirred panels, framed by anything-but-skimpy celadon silk curtains gathered at chair-rail height.

More intimate is the upstairs sitting room, the perfect place for having a drink before dinner, watching television, or warming up by the fire. "We are all influenced by what has been done in the past whenever we create something," says Spectre. "The challenge is to use it as a departure point, to enhance it. I think that's what real design is about. It doesn't have to be completely original." Thus said, Spectre's tour de force is the Art Deco–inspired fireplace wall of elm burl and brushed bronze, which conceals both a wet bar and television. "We could have done something that looked consistent with the architecture, but the clients wanted us to do something different, to make our mark in a more lasting way," he says, obviously pleased at their choice. The beauty of the burnished wood grain is complemented by other equally tempting surfaces: leather, soft suede, scagliola. The cohesive use of dark cognac makes the atmosphere even cozier, and suede upholstery — "the color of the inside of a plum" — on the chairs picks up the cool bronze detailing of the new wall unit.

Four seventeenth-century armchairs, Ming lacquer table, Oushak rug, and Arman sculpture are just a few of the precious pieces in the generously proportioned living room.

Spectre's showstopping fireplace wall of elm burl and brushed bronze conceals a bar and media wall.

Spectre's talent for blending the best of the past and the present is revealed in another house, a 1940s Connecticut manor that he decorated from scratch. Rarely is a designer presented with an empty house to fill with furniture and objets d'art, as Spectre was here. He began by determining the mood the owners were seeking for their new home — "not too modern, not too conventional." Fortunately, there was much to respect both in the integrity of the architecture and in the lush surroundings, twenty-two acres of rolling meadows.

Inspired by the outdoors, Spectre had a geranium chintz custom-colored for the living room. To unify this large space, Spectre used it everywhere — on matching sofas and armchairs, arranged in two different conversation areas, and at the bay windows and French doors. All the custom-designed furniture is quilted and overstuffed for extra comfort. Intense red, probably the only color that could hold its own amid this floral extravaganza, pops up throughout the room in bold accent pieces: a Chinese lacquer screen, a late-nineteenth-century Heriz rug, a cinnabar tray table, silk pillows. With this jubilee of pattern and color, Spectre decided to keep the shell of the room intentionally subtle: His design of the white-oak fireplace wall and mantel is a simplified update of a classic paneled treatment.

The lively geranium chintz living room punctuated with cinnabar screens and Okulick wall sculpture.

For the dining room, Spectre looked again to strong, bright hues. He had the walls lacquered red, a painstaking and expensive process but one that yields an unrivaled luster. Spectre installed a paneled dado in the style of the original pine woodwork and painted it white; it is a cool relief from the hot tone of the paint above it. So are the pale stenciled floor and white-oak table a foil for the dark mahogany of the Regency side cabinet and George III chairs. Blue-and-white garniture, as majestic as towering sculptures, and an eighteenth-century Japanese screen with its pure greens and golds complete the sizzle of color here.

In the library Spectre hung one of two paintings by an artist, George Deem, whose vernacular he likes. It pays homage to the French surrealist Magritte. "I think their combination of word and image defines the greater part of the twentieth century," says Spectre, who likes the painting as a transition between the old and the new. "I don't think a picture has to go with a room. I think it goes with a mood and an attitude. There is no one picture for one particular spot."

The lacquered red dining room is a perfect foil for the exquisite blue and white porcelain collection.

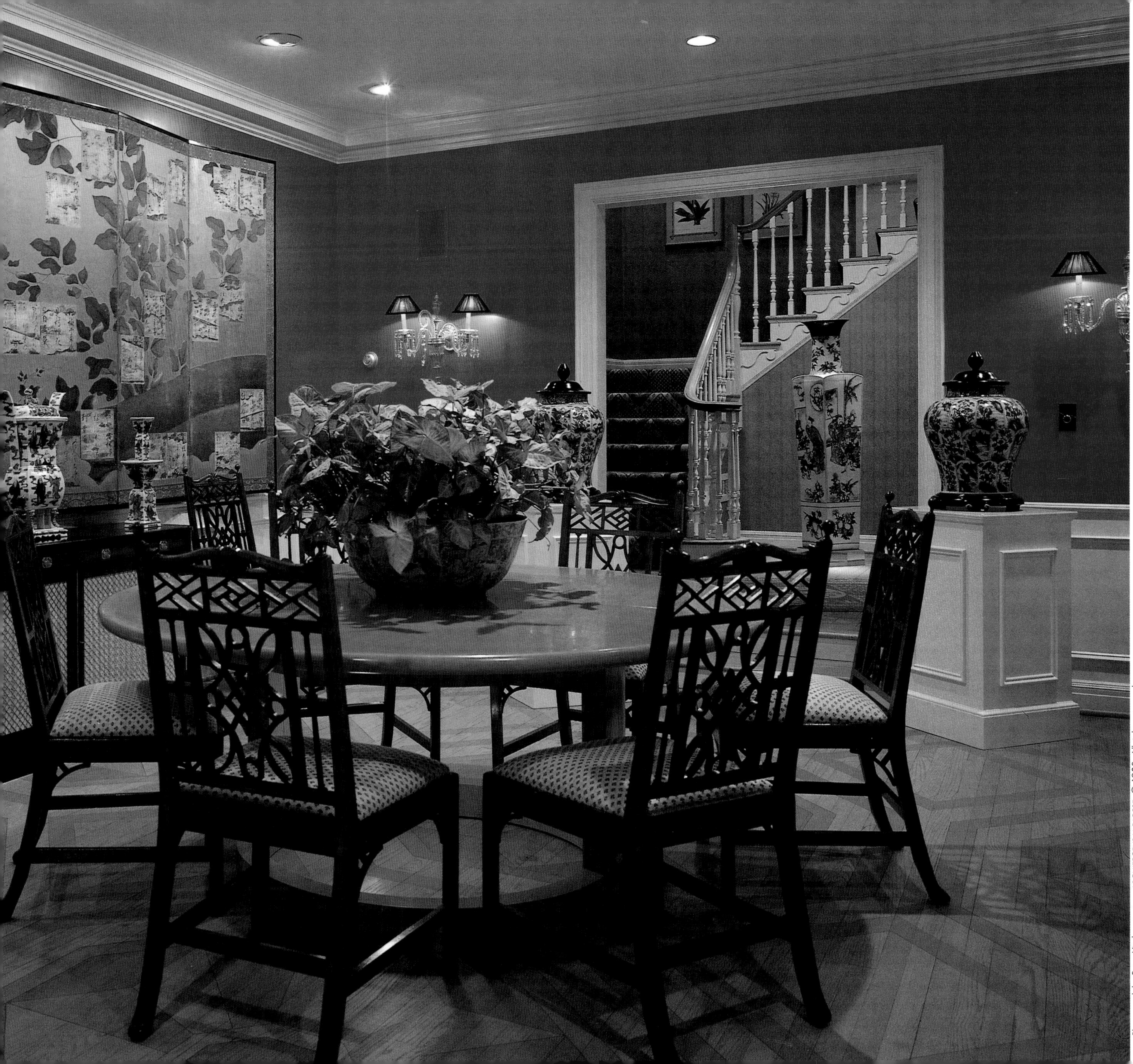

Spectre chose a softer palette for the interior of a modern stucco, stone, and glass structure in Mexico City. Inside its walls a quiet calm prevails, a feeling deliberately invoked by its decorator, Spectre. "I believe it is essential to some people to have some serenity in their personal lives," says Spectre. "We try to achieve this serenity through a certain softness of design, through convenient furniture arrangements, through colors that are pleasing to the eye and flattering to the occupant, and through technology which has become a source of great comfort in our daily lives."

The large house was built around a courtyard, its plaza paved with an antique Roman mosaic. Glass walls, which can be opened for entertaining under the stars, incorporate this atrium into the enlarged open-plan living room.

The palatial entrance to a Mexico City residence of extraordinary proportions.

Spectre upholstered the walls in taupe
ultra-suede, saddle-stitched in square blocks
in imitation of real suede to give it a sculptural
relief. A carpet in similar colors unifies the
spacious room; Oriental rugs and a rug by
Giacometti anchor the different conversation
groupings. Spectre also chose soft tones for
the silks covering the furniture he custom-
designed. "Background and texture are
paramount to the way I think about
decoration," he says. "The prints and
textures in the room are all subtle. They don't
compete with art, and I knew that these
people were collectors and would become
even more serious about collecting as time
went on."

A corner of the expansive reception area
with a Tamayo painting over the sofa.

A museum-quality
Toulouse-Lautrec
painting of a
Montmartre scene
against taupe mohair
velvet walls.

A spare but
super-elegant
drawing room
featuring a
Maillol bronze,
Flora, Nude,
Giacometti table
and rug, and
Regency antique
bamboo chairs.

In Fox Chapel, outside Pittsburgh, a house built in the twenties for the Hellmann family became, in Spectre's skillful hands, a dramatic showplace for the new owners' collection of contemporary art. Says Spectre: "The grounds and architecture were really very beautiful. I was reminded of an older Bel Air or Beverly Hills mansion updated in the Art Deco style. We followed that influence throughout the house."

Spectre designed the new forecourt and entrance anteroom, which he felt were important to boost the integrity of the house. "The house needed a more impressive approach, a certain air of distinction that was lacking," he says. He added the bronze pumas that flank the front door.

90

ABOVE

A pair of pumas guard the anteroom.

RIGHT

The impressive facade of a Pittsburgh mansion at twilight showing Spectre's distinctive forecourt.

The central hall, like the sun-filled corridor that runs the length of the house, is really a gallery for art. White veined marble, a new Giacometti-motif iron rail for the sweeping staircase, and pearl-gray paint on the walls provide an updated Deco setting for pieces like the whimsical sculpture by Jeff Koons. The curve of the console table designed by Spectre was inspired by the shape of the original balcony railings visible just outside the French doors. It also echoes the oval canvas by Jerry Brane.

The gallery corridor that unites the principal living areas.

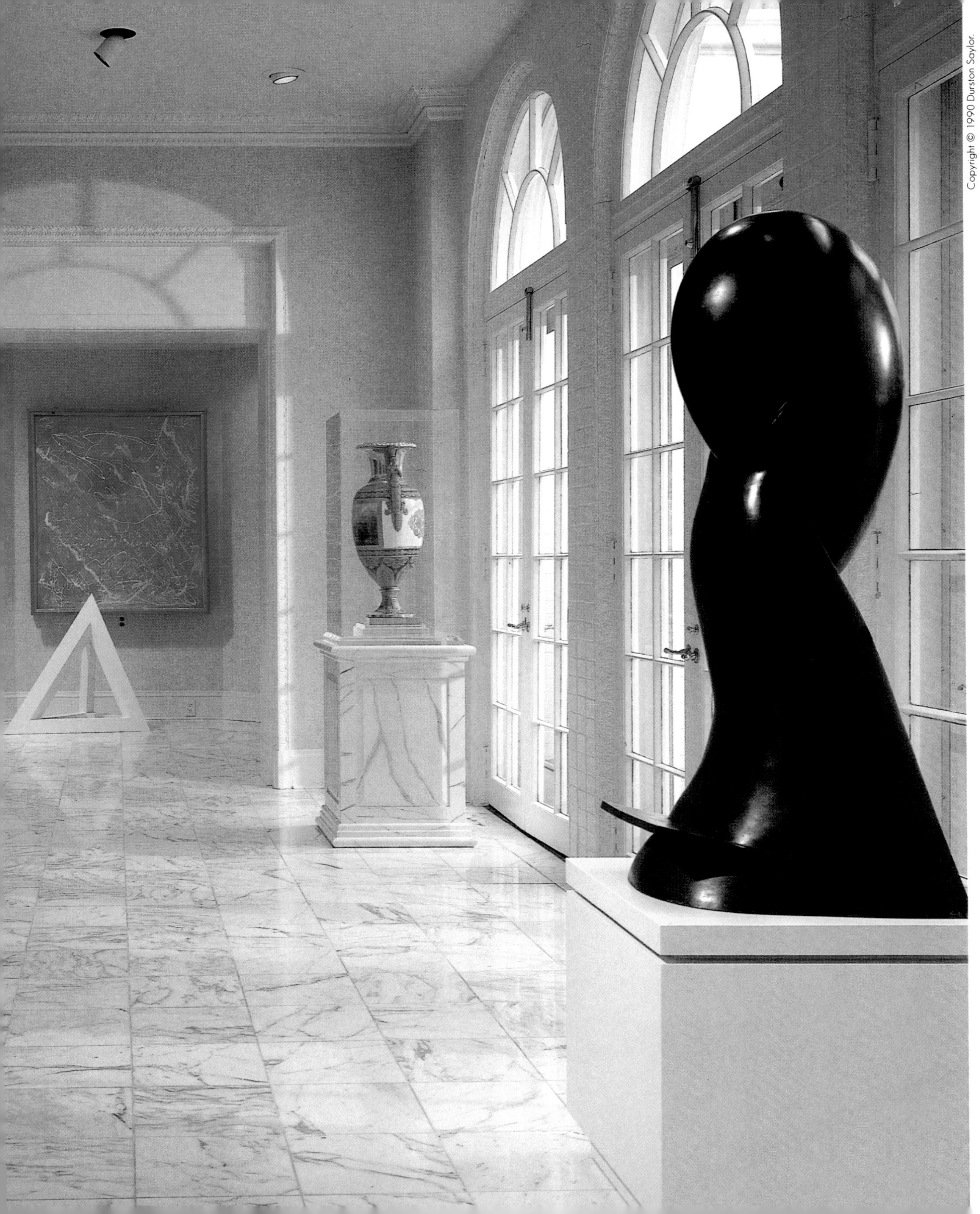

94

The Jeff Koons
sculpture at the
foot of the staircase
in the double-volume
central hall.

A concurrence of curves
—the Jerry Brane canvas,
Spectre custom-designed table,
and Giacometti rug.

The inviting atmosphere of the living room was created with the mellow, luminous cast of the pervasive pale, buttery yellow: of the silk-upholstered walls and in the late-nineteenth-century Chinese rug. There are no fussy elements here. The decoration is underlined by comfortable seating pieces upholstered in taupe tones and a soft window treatment in the same silk as the walls. Period echoes in the original marble mantel and woodwork provide a framework for the owners' ever-expanding collection of art, here primarily American and European works from the last decade.

Interesting contrasts: the Jay Spectre steel-and-glass coffee table on a nineteenth-century Chinese rug.

Fireplace and triangle painting by Robert Mangold.

A view from the central hall through the pale yellow living room.

Unlike many a formal dining room where stuffiness is the rule, this may be the most playful room in the house, thanks to the overall tone of the art on display. Serving up at least one laugh is Gary Mirabelle's sculpture of an English butler, whose appeal has since inspired the artist to create a French maid. Equally eye-catching is the furniture based on pieces by the Art Deco master Emile-Jacques Ruhlmann. The chairs, covered in luscious raspberry horsehide, are in richly grained Macassar ebony, as is the dining table. Even the original moldings are finished to resemble this opulent wood. An Art Deco chandelier and a Sonia Delaunay pattern on the walls complete this vintage look. "You wouldn't be surprised if I told you these people entertain constantly, would you?" remarks Spectre.

RIGHT

A dining table that can seat up to twenty-four people when extended is the center of this whimsically appointed room.

LEFT

The subtle palette of Imi Knoebel's pink, white, and red oil is echoed by the upholstery.

Another twenties house, this one in
Westchester, New York, demanded an
entirely different approach. The traditional
stone manor-house architecture, the task of a
complete renovation, and the huge scale of
the 25,000-square-foot house were among
the influential factors here. Working with an
architect, Spectre restored the house to its
former grandeur. "Between the time the
house was built and our client purchased it,
it had been torn apart and modernized in
a very unfortunate fashion," says Spectre.
Because no record of the original front
facade existed, a new entrance was
designed that would respect the house's
integrity yet also reflect his own point of view.
The door is crafted of thick etched-glass
panels, rather than wooden ones, to take
advantage of the clear view through the
house to the lake.

A creative approach was needed for the
landscape architecture. A steep slope from
the rear of the house to the eight-acre park
required some sort of transition. A big loggia
on the side of the house and overlooking the
pool ruled out the need for a straight terrace,
so a more innovative solution was achieved:
graceful lawned steps that gently break the
hill into manageable strides.

100

From the drive
approaching Greystone Manor,
overlooked by a stacked stone
sculpture, *Asenat and Josef*,
by Boaz Vaadia.

Equally challenging was the decoration of the entrance hall. The oppressive red-brown stain of the staircase hid its delicate hand-carving, so Spectre bleached the millwork, then picked out the details and reiterated them in a custom-designed wallpaper. A carpet, also of his design, completes the new look, now very contemporary. Enormous stereo speakers posed a problem as well. Spectre had open latticework cabinets built to house them that would also serve as pedestals for each of a pair of Loane figures.

One of a pair of life-size Loane figures that grace the living room.

Original hand-carved mill work at the foot of the stairs.

An inviting corner of the living room.

A wide range of fabrics and textures was arrayed in the living room, a space large enough to handle many decorative elements, to give the luxurious feel the clients wanted in their formal entertaining area. To create an unobtrusive background, Spectre wrapped the walls in upholstered neutral-toned raw silk and covered the floor with a pale gray-and-cream floral rug. The soft setting absorbs the Art Deco pattern on the club chairs, bottle-green silk on the quilted pillows, leather on the sofas, chintz on the window-seat banquette with a lullaby ease. Of exceptional quality are the early-nineteenth-century Japanese tables of carved cinnabar and the gilt Regency mirror above the restored stone mantel. Spectre picked it for its immense scale and for its bulrush motifs, which reminded him of those growing on the property's lake.

A B O V E

Detail of a highly unusual nineteenth-century grandfather clock in the entrance hall.

R I G H T

Detail of the gilt Regency mirror that dominates the living room.

The landscaped steps.

BELOW

Chevron white-oak floors provide a subtle backdrop
for a collection of English and Oriental pieces.

Electricians discovered the library's barrel-arched ceiling, which had been concealed in a past remodeling, when they went to install the lighting. Spectre was thrilled and embellished this architectural asset by stenciling little stars in silver and gold onto it for whimsical starry nights. So that the owners could observe the real celestial heavens, a telescope stands ready beside one of a wall of French doors opening onto the grounds. Among Spectre's treasure trove of finds are the Oriental desk bought in Paris, the Tiffany lamp, the nineteenth-century chair. Against the restored dark wood paneling, a Japanese screen of marionettes is especially fresh and colorful.

"When a house is as large as this one, you have to make sure its occupants won't be eaten up by all the space," says Spectre. His solution in the dining room was to install doors for more intimacy. Not that they close you in. Glass allows the room to be enjoyed by passersby in the massive corridor that runs through the house. There is a distinct airy quality to the interior here, a result of the spare furnishings and the pale oak floor in a chevron parquet. Spectre chose dark green mohair velvet for the walls and Queen Anne–style chairs. "It seemed compatible with what we were doing everywhere else, and it's a very pleasant color to dine in," he says. Spectre, who has his own line of tableware, is very sensitive to the way design affects an appreciation of food.

RIGHT

A paneled library opens onto the
terraced lawn.

5. EXTRAVAGANT ESCAPES

The great getaway. We all dream about it. Perhaps it's a lakeside fishing lodge or a sun-filled bungalow by the beach. Wherever and whatever it is, that second home is all about relaxation. "It's only when you reach a certain point in life that you realize just how valuable qualities such as harmony and repose are," says Jay Spectre, contemplating his country house in New Canaan, Connecticut.

This client's cherished retreat is situated on the slopes of Vail, Colorado. "There are many things here that intentionally suggest we're in the middle of the country geographically, not in some jet-set never-never land," he says. "I was seeking a liberated, relaxed atmosphere, away from the formality of society but still terribly elegant." For starters, there is the massive scale of the house (assembled from two smaller connected houses on the site) that is somehow perfectly suited to the mountains and sweeping horizon of Colorado. The gigantic pitched roof — a natural choice given all the snow — fits into the landscape of peaks. The skylights open up the main living and dining room, making it a part of the outdoors, not just a fortress against it. A stucco chimney breast with a rounded opening for the fireplace is "adobe-like, very Native American" in Spectre's eyes. Equally evocative of the West and its frontier history are the Frederick Remington bronze figures, the duck decoys, and the chamois suede covering the sofas and chairs.

Installing a steep white-oak-paneled ceiling, Spectre played a visual game in the design of the living room, setting the window next to the fireplace at an angle up the wall and the two sections that make up the coffee table on the diagonal. "Geometry has always supplied the underlying harmony in my spaces," says Spectre.

"Everything in the room is overscale, so that although it's an enormous room, there's not a lot of furniture," says Spectre. "The colors — saddle leather, blues, whites, celadon greens — go with the landscape. They have a wonderful feeling of the outside as well as the inside. After all, the house is right on the ski slope."

A soaring ceiling is anchored
by a pair of brushed-steel columns in
this luxurious retreat.

ABOVE

A Remington bronze Indian in the living room
gazes over the spectacular ski slopes.

RIGHT

A view of the dramatic drawing room
in the Colorado retreat.

112

Part of the fun of a vacation house is having recreational rooms like this billiards room, which Spectre carved out of what was wasted space in the interior of the house. Pool is a big draw after a day of skiing. Making up for the absence of a window is the warm glow of the canvas-covered walls and ceiling, which were handpainted, not to imitate a particular surface, but to lend texture and richness to the small room. In each corner illuminated vitrines display pool sticks. Like almost all the furniture in the house, the pool table was custom-made.

The master bedroom was also excavated from unused space, this time in the roof area of the house, which explains the different ceiling planes dropped to cope with plumbing and air ducts. "The upholstered bed treatment is one of our best looks: It's classic, comfortable, easily maintained, and very twentieth century," he says. An Hermès fox throw, luxurious and eminently practical in the alpine climate, is sure to keep the owners warm while they watch the television that lifts hydraulically — at the touch of a button in the built-in nightstand — from the Oriental-style chest at the foot of the bed.

LEFT

The pool room in the heart of the house, with an exceptional pair of Japanese screens depicting a pride of lions.

RIGHT

A warm retreat from the snowy slopes. Custom Spectre lamps shed soft light on the salmon cotton walls. The lacquer chest conceals a television set that rises to eye level at the push of a button.

ABOVE

Dramatic marble floor treatment and aged
fresco walls in the entrance gallery.

LEFT

Looking across the living room through
the sliding doors at Key Biscayne.

In southern climes, the intensity of the sun affects the designer's palette. Why? Because color is actually just the reflection of light waves. "The light changes in various parts of the world," says Spectre. "I've seen persimmon and orange shades that look wonderful in Italy, so-so in New York, and beautiful in Bel Air or Key West. I've seen colors change in an eighteenth-century carpet and I've seen them change on the exteriors of houses." Compound this with the festive attitude of resort communities (just think of the sometimes outlandish resort collections shown each winter by the fashion designers), and it seems only natural that Spectre would choose bright, bold colors when decorating in Florida and Jamaica.

For a South American couple who are wine connoisseurs and equestrians, Spectre designed a wintertime retreat in Miami using the vivid palette favored by the glamorous wife. Creating interest in the architecturally limited apartment required ingenuity and creative solutions. A dramatic improvement was the installation of a new floor in the thirty-foot stretch of entrance hall. Its simple geometry adds structural interest to the long corridor, its veined marble a little luxury. "We had it cut in Carrara, Italy, and shipped over in pieces," says Spectre. "We really needed something exciting here to give the area a lift." Picking up the blue and green tones of the stone is the fresco wall treatment, handpainted in panels in Italy. Their luminous sea-green glaze was inspired by the cool water of Biscayne Bay, which the apartment overlooks.

In other places too Spectre captured the feeling of the ocean. The living room is opened on two sides to terraced balconies. "I really like sliding glass doors," says Spectre. "There's nothing as practical or luxurious or complimentary to a view. I'm sure the inspiration comes from 2,000-year-old houses in Japan with those shoji screens. Although they are somewhat cliché in building standards, they function very well."

Spectre went for a look of cool simplicity in the living room with a few carefully chosen comfortable pieces in solid saturated hues. A blue cotton in an undulating wavelike pattern covers the sofas. "It echoes the movement of the sea," explains Spectre. Plump pillows in pistachio green and lemon silk are lush accents. "I arranged the furniture on the diagonal to make a more compelling statement," he says. This decorating idea works especially well in square rooms like this where the architecture is truly uninspired, as well as in large rooms that possess a bit more structure. A pair of Moderne-style armchairs are zipped up with leather strip-quilting. "I like Art Deco references in this city where the later kitsch style flourished," says Spectre. "I've known Miami and Miami Beach since I was a child. I used to stay at the great Art Deco hotels — the Normandie, the New Yorker — long before they were restored." The room's anchor, surprisingly the last thing chosen for the room, is a deep blue nineteenth-century Chinese rug.

115

116

The rich grain and caramel tone of tamo, a rare wood forested in Japan, lends substance to the multifunctional sitting room. "I like the texture of it," says Spectre. "It has the feeling of water or moiré, which meshes wonderfully with an environment that is surrounded by water." An array of deep, strong colors — rust, teal — stand up to the resonant wood paneling of the media wall unit and desk. Here, Spectre positioned the banquette so one could take in both the television and the bay view, disturbed only by a swiveling armchair. Spectre mixed strong materials — brick, marble, leather — with the exotic tamo for a balanced feeling of relaxed comfort. The pillows — leather on one side, cotton on the other — are "quilted like a Chanel bag for interest," according to Spectre.

Like many master bedrooms, this one was decorated with the wife, not the husband, in mind. He will put up with it, she will love it. "She wanted a colorful, feminine bedroom," says Spectre. "Some husbands can adjust to this. They feel that it is their wife's room. In other instances women want the room more tailored and feel that their husband will be more comfortable. They're all correct." With bedrooms, the designer feels, the decoration has more to do with finishes, colors, and patterns than with any novel arrangement of furniture because the function is predetermined. The two paintings inspired the rainbow of silk checks on the upholstered bed, armchair, and ottoman. A typical Spectre twist is the pink walls, not as prettily prim as they seem at first glance: They are painted in a subtle sharkskin pattern.

117

ABOVE

The master bedroom
reflected in
an English
nineteenth-century
shell mirror.

LEFT

The faux book-lined doors of the media cabinet
pocket back to reveal the large television
screen and stereo equipment.

In the Palm Beach high-rise buildings that line the waterfront, the interior architecture is usually forgettable, the ocean view quite the opposite. For one client, Spectre returned to a decorating trick he frequently uses in Manhattan apartments: He mirrored the side walls to expand the room visually and to reflect the spectacular seascape. The living room, a shell of white on white, harks back to the glamorous "white telephone" look of early Hollywood sets. *Dinner at Eight* with Jean Harlow comes to mind; the eleven shades of white used in this Art Deco arena caused quite a stir. A white piano from the twenties is more than a vaudevillian period accent: the wife, a very talented singer, loves to entertain friends and family. The sofas, banquette, and armchairs are upholstered in deeply textured cotton, and the bleached-oak floor is covered by two area rugs, all in various vanilla tones.

Spectre says the interior could be any color. "With an apartment right on the ocean the light changes hour to hour," he says. "White seemed to be a complement to the setting."

Set within this cool, comfortable oasis under the glimmer of Art Deco–style light fixtures are opulent Oriental cloisonné vases and cinnabar lamps, large twentieth-century European paintings, colorful striped pillows. "Nothing is too matched up," says Bradfield. "It's more interesting this way." Two lacquered wicker chairs trimmed in gold and ivory — copies of the Brighton Pavilion classics that the designers found in Hong Kong — are pulled up to a rattan-and-glass card table. "Our work comprises many cultures and many periods," says Spectre. "For this couple it is important that when everything comes together, the interiors should say now — very twentieth century."

Spectre likes to build on affinities between furnishings and art. A marvelous example is in the master bedroom, where the checkerboard pattern of the silk, upholstered on the bed, is picked up in the background of a Ben Schonzeit canvas. This is matching Spectre-style. Oddly enough, the fabric was picked out long before the painting was found. Spectre's intended evocation of a way of living between the two world wars gives this room a quiet glamour so perfect for Palm Beach.

A witty composition of
art, furnishings, and accessories
set against a backdrop of
off-white serenity.

118

A musical corner
showing an upright piano
commissioned for the
1939 World's Fair.
Two cinnabar lamps
light the foreground.

The master bedroom fabric and painting express a harlequin twist.

A treasure trove of collectibles suspended above the ocean.

Another penthouse, this one on Breakers Row in Palm Beach, reveals a similarly laid-back approach to the decorating: Let the view do the work. "When you have the good fortune to be right on the ocean — the trees, the views, the beach — it definitely influences the interior environment," says Spectre. The L-shaped living room curls around a spacious porch; floor-to-ceiling glass doors bring the outdoors inside. Spectre felt a pale setting was the best way to set off the owners' lovingly collected objects and works of art and to emphasize the spectacular beach view. "This couple has a great flair for life, an amusing approach that they bring to a room," he says. "In their case the room really becomes an accessory to their personality. They don't require a lot of decoration."

Instead of bright white, Spectre chose a muted palette from the sand and sea: a soft blue-green for the rug, with a plush border inspired by the coastline; off-white walls; bleached wood floors; a custom-colored dark-green-on-white floral print for the furniture. Says its designer: "It reminded me of French Impressionist drawings and of artists that I've always admired like Verte (he did the walls at the Café Carlyle). It had an almost thirties or forties approach to decoration. I often like prints that are only one color, because they look like drawings or sketches." Each upholstered piece is over-stuffed for comfort's sake.

Echoing the striking silhouette of the floral fabric are the iron creations of Diego Giacometti: two glass-topped tables and a coat rack simulated to look like a tree, with its branchlike arms and sitting owl. A special-commission étagère by the artist is host to a collection of pre-Columbian figures. "There was no need for the introduction of any architecture after we brought in these iron pieces," says Spectre.

Giacometti's étagère in bronze houses a collection of pre-Columbian clay figures.

In the master bedroom, Spectre used a lush cotton print throughout to give a sense of serenity and cohesion. "The pattern is from a seventeenth-century Venetian document," says Spectre. "That's amazing to me because it feels so stunningly modern." An upholstered chaise by the window is a perfect spot for catching a quiet glimpse of the crashing waves. "This private little corner conveys the meaning of escape," says Spectre. Perhaps in homage to Florida sunroom style, Spectre designed a mirrored fretwork media wall unit.

LEFT

A Macassar ebony dining table inspired by Emile-Jacques Ruhlmann beneath Cheret's alabaster and bronze chandelier.

RIGHT

A custom-upholstered chaise in an intimate corner of the bedroom.

A relaxed look was the aim in Spectre's redesign of an East Hampton weekend house, which had already been well appointed by another top decorator. "The house is made for parties," says Spectre. "It's a beach house in every sense of the word." A long and not particularly impressive entrance is energized with a peppy mint-green paint job. "It just seemed the right mood for a resort home," he says. Nothing is too serious here. The hooked-rug wall hanging is a whimsical bird's-eye view of the Long Island coast.

Also in the lighthearted spirit is Alan Siegel's chair sculpture; it looks something like a cello, and its placement in the living room next to the grand piano emphasizes the resemblance. The decoration is minimal: wall-to-wall off-white carpeting for padding around on in bare feet, wide-open glass walls, off-white painted walls, a pitched ceiling paneled in oak planks. A Ben Schonzeit painting of a tree, hung on the wall in a corner, mimics the nearby view, a double-take effect that makes Spectre chuckle.

"The whole house is geared to indoor-outdoor living," says Spectre. Sliding glass doors open the sitting room onto the beautiful sweep of green lawn, dunes, and blue water. Spectre opted for wicker chairs here, picking up the color of the ocean in their cushions and in a beach-scene painting above the sand-toned leather love seat. He chose whitewashed oak for the partial wall here (and for the ceiling of the adjacent room), which relates to the porch. It is quite a sight when the occupants arrive by helicopter on the back lawn. They also own a Gulfstream jet, the interior of which Spectre designed.

The dining room, a large space with a strong rectilinear emphasis, is pulled together with a pair of circa-1880 Japanese screens, a favorite technique in the Spectre repertoire. The designer balanced the hard-edged articulation of the window molding with an upholstered-panel wall treatment, here in salmon-colored moiré silk. "The unity is derived from the interplay of soft hues, textures, and silhouettes," he explains.

ABOVE

One aspect of the expansive East Hampton living room with Alan Siegel's whimsical sculpture *White Eyes.*

LEFT

A pair of Japanese screens of the royal stables frame this salmon-colored dining room, which opens onto a private courtyard.

Speed was of the essence in the decoration of a newly expanded house on the grounds of Jamaica's exclusive Tryall Club. Spectre and Bradfield saw the residence for the first time in September; the owners, for whom Spectre has completed several other projects, including their yacht, wanted to be in by Christmas. The time crunch eliminated the possibility of having any furniture custom-designed. Nearly all the pieces are from Spectre's furniture line for Century.

The international couple was attracted to the designer's vernacular for its inspired use of Oriental *objets*. More appropriate here, felt Spectre, would be to use the local decorative art — carved wooden animals, handpainted ceramics — as a recurring accent. Equally responsive to the indigenous culture was the choice of strong, clear colors. "They are pungent," says Spectre. "We used lots of white as a counterpoint." Spectre welcomed the aesthetic input of his clients. "This always makes a job easier and faster," he says. "The wife has a wonderful visual sensibility. They both really love the island, and I think it shows in the house."

Built around a pool courtyard, "Linger Longer," as the house is named, backs up to the Tryall golf course. Three Caribbean-style fluted hurricane roofs give it a dramatic silhouette from the beach beyond. An expansive wraparound porch forms a wonderful outdoor living area; plantation shutters at the windows (there is no glass) open up the interior to the cool island breezes. "It's a very natural form of air conditioning," says Bradfield. "Very few people have glazing on windows."

129

The dramatic evening profile of the house at Tryall.

The great room is truly great, measuring, as it does, sixty feet long, with an octagonal bay on the sea side. A cotton chintz, alive with monkeys leaping over and under intertwining vines, is tropical in feeling. Spectre used it in off-white for the curtains and in black on matching sofas. An octagonal carpet in the bay sitting area ties the various colors together. In other parts of the room and throughout the house, the floor is intentionally bare for a cooler feeling. That is not to say it is plain: Purple heartwood, forested in Brazil, radiates underfoot.

The charming entryway to "Linger Longer," a house on the grounds of Jamaica's Tryall Club.

Spectre's custom-designed woodwork delineates the wraparound porch.

Looking through the slouchy yet sophisticated great room out to sea.

132

Geared to entertaining, the room also hosts a large dining table. A gamut of harlequin-inspired hues runs around it on the upholstered seats of Spectre's rattan chairs. "Purple, coral, jade — the whole house is filled with these colors," says Spectre. Pumping up the intensity of color not only fits in with the ebullient palette of the island's landscape but also gives the Spectre Collection furniture a unique daring. An example of how his furniture looks very custom is his Wallis chair and ottoman in raspberry linen damask in one of the guest rooms. "The pieces marry wonderfully with the lattice railing of the porch," says Spectre. "That's because they share an overriding classicism."

A quintessentially tropical place setting.

The clean-cut dining area with access to the pool.

The "Wallis" chairs glow against the purple heartwood floors that run throughout the house.

Spectre's channeled ottoman and chaise longue invite elegant lounging in the master bedroom.

6. MARKETING A LIFESTYLE

Jay Spectre enjoys marketing almost as much as designing. Together with his creative and business partner, Geoffrey Bradfield, he originates a wide variety of beautifully designed products from the elegant but functional offices in midtown Manhattan. From the moment you enter the reception area you know you're in expert hands. Glorious pre-Columbian jars line the windowsill in the hall, waiting for the perfect niche. Drawings of Spectre classics are framed on the walls. The conference room is sleek, comfortable, and efficient, with celadon steamer chairs grouped around an Eclipse table. It opens into Jay's office, a pocket marvel with Spanish Renaissance carved chairs upholstered in green brocade and an Eclipse desk.

LEFT

Jay Spectre and Geoffrey Bradfield, national publicity for the DIFFA showhouse, *Metropolitan Home*.

ABOVE

The entrance to the Spectre office, showing a range of signature materials and texture contrasts, wild oak, stone floors, upholstered walls, and white metal.

RIGHT

Jay Spectre's private office. His desk and étagères from his own Eclipse collection, two Italian seventeenth-century chairs, and a Braque drawing on the wall provide a serene setting in a hectic business.

The Eclipse table (and desk, armchair, and end table) were the mainstay of Spectre's first collection for Century Furniture, launched in spring 1986. Luckily he enjoys chatting, selling and promoting his point of view, because he was thrust in front of a roomful of people with questions about the line. His presentation to the design media was brief. "I'd like to introduce my Eclipse table. The oak top features two inlaid circles intersecting one another, eclipsing one another, which is where the name came from. This is one of the first examples of using lasers in making furniture. You could call it high-tech marquetry. The curve of the inlay for the table top is charted by computer, then the laser cuts the inlay and the channel for it in the tabletop, yielding an almost perfect fit. The base of the table is steel, four strong steel legs supporting a stylized globe in the center, which represents the world. I think the table is a classic."

He was right. By the end of two weeks in North Carolina, Spectre was acknowledged as a designer with popular potential. The sales of the line reflected its appeal. Spectre had found a niche in the market for a softer-edged, less clinical line of furniture: stylish, clean, and comfortable. In 1990 Bloomingdale's honored Spectre for creating the best-selling contemporary furniture line in its history.

Jay Spectre brought years of experience and ideas to this new design venture. His affinity for contemporary furniture began early on while working for Cornelius Hubbuch, a pioneer in the business, and continued as he stocked and sold from his first boutique furnishings store in Louisville. He kept a mental diary of ideas, and after years of designing custom pieces for his exclusive clientele, he was confident that he could

ABOVE

Eclipse table with round-back armchairs.

TOP RIGHT

Eclipse desk or vanity table with swivel stool.

BOTTOM RIGHT

Eclipse end table.

LEFT

The conference room. The Eclipse table and steamer chairs are dominated by George Deem's painting *School of Bauhaus.* The back wall conceals a state-of-the-art media panel for presentations.

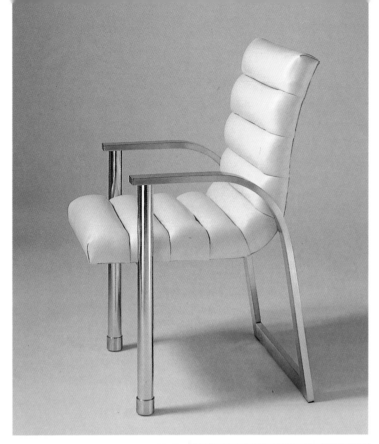

give a wide range of people just what they wanted. Says Spectre: "I've always thought people should try to live as well as they try to look. I want to help the greatest number of people possible achieve beautifully decorated space, because in my opinion decorating can be a matter of life and death. As Oscar Wilde lay dying on his bed, he raised himself up on one elbow, looked around, and said, 'This wallpaper is killing me. Either it goes or I go.' And with that Mr. Wilde went."

What really set Spectre apart was his point of view, a certain approach to design that was clearly missing in the furniture showrooms of America. In the eighties, according to Carl Levine, senior vice president of Bloomingdale's, "there was a great upsurge in demand for better-quality modern furniture. The American market wasn't paying much attention to that classification.

"Jay has a keen sense of style in his whole presence: in the way he dresses and in the way he lives. His designs are contemporary and original, yet they have strong antecedents in the early-twentieth-century design of Art Deco." This classical quality, this intellectual attitude toward furnishing, is what makes his work special. Says Levine: "The design is very appealing without being challenging. It's not high-tech or Memphis, where the whole personality of a room changes if you bring in one chair. It looks classic, which means in the eyes of a sophisticated customer it will last a long time. It's not trendy."

A B O V E

Three lamps from a series of thirty-six Spectre designed for Paul Hanson.
Bradfield went to Moradabad, mining capital of India, to oversee their production.

L E F T

A pair of classics: The Eclipse dining chair and lounge chair.

Levine forged the business relationship between Spectre and Century Furniture Company, with Bloomingdale's getting an exclusive in its regional markets. The foundation for what turned out to be a sixty-six-piece debut line (the triad had been shooting for somewhere between a dozen and fifteen) came from an inventory of prototypes and custom designs that Spectre had developed over his long career. "We expanded upon what we do the best and like the most — the twentieth century according to me," he says. Oak, steel, and leather were combined in strong sculptural pieces designed to endure both wear and tear and the swings of fashion. "One of the goals we set was that this furniture not just satisfy snob appeal or my own egomania or be a critical success with no sales. We wanted the furniture sales people at Bloomingdale's to want to own a piece of our furniture, and they did and they do." That's not to say it isn't top-notch quality. Spectre uses furniture from the Century collection, sometimes as much as 25 percent of the total furniture, in interiors for clients, as well as in his two homes. "Doing this makes the overall price tag of a job a little more palatable," he says.

The designer-label mystique, so powerful in the retail worlds of fashion and fragrance, certainly has had something to do with Spectre's overwhelming commercial success. "There is a great prestige to buying a Jay Spectre piece of furniture because he's been identified with the custom-design world for so long," says Levine. "And here you're able to buy a piece of this world at department store prices."

East Side/West Side.
This name began as a
New York neighborhood tease
but came to have
more international
connotations.

In designing furniture, Spectre mines the same sources he does when decorating, looking not to the Regency or Empire periods but to this century for inspiration. There is a sense of nostalgia rather than history revisited. Says Spectre: "Now that we are looking into the twenty-first century, the great designs of our century have been validated as worthy decorative inspiration. My designs are about the earth, the universe, and what we've experienced in this era." Spectre staples — the steamer chair, the deep channeled sofa — were instant hits.

"I try to tell people where my design idea came from," says Spectre. "I think that has a great deal to do with its appeal. The stories that come with each piece of furniture are very real to me." He brings the make-believe world of old Hollywood movies to life in many of his pieces: the oh-so-soft scallop-back "Lombard" sofa; the Goddess chair with its spiraling sweep of a back; the Harlow chaise; the open-back chair named "Rear Window" after Hitchcock's memorable film. Even more literal and playful is his "Joan Crawford" table with its shiny red top shaped like the actress's mouth. Furniture has never been as whimsical and seductive.

The Joan Crawford table is a surrealist statement—an impression of the star's lips from her famous movie *Mildred Pierce*. The color of the top is from a Chanel lipstick called "Star Red."

"Rear Window" chair.

The era inspired Spectre to create the "Wallis" chair, named for the legendary Duchess of Windsor, whose personal style and daring were inimitable. He indulged his taste for the dramatic (and that of his customers) with other unusual but still accessible pieces. Take the "Entrance Maker" console: its ziggurat-shaped front support recalls the step-back form of an Art Deco skyscraper. The clever double message in its name promises that it will spike the client's entrance with movie star glamour and reflect that glamour on the client as well.

Most of the wooden furniture was introduced in white oak with some pieces available in the ebony finish "Glorious Cinematic Black and White." "The idea for white oak came out of a new attitude toward decoration: happier, lighter in feeling," says Spectre. "I had seen a great deal of blond-oak furniture in the south of France many years ago. I remember the doors at the Hôtel du Cap there were so beautiful. I tried it in my own apartment and found it easy to live with. I like the combination of the strength of the oak and the cheerful look of the pale finish." When Buck Shuford, president of Century Furniture, suggested brass instead of steel for the hardware as a way of expanding the collection's appeal to include a more tradition-oriented audience, Spectre balked. "That's not my point of view."

Spectre added cognac ash burl, a shade as resonant as aged brandy, in 1987 and maple and primavera woods finished in "suede" (light tan bordering on pale peach) in 1991. "I think it's very much today's color," he says. Levine says that the finish is "softer, more in tune with the understatement of the nineties."

"Entrance Maker" console.

Wicker and rattan move off the back porch and into the house in Spectre's hands, translated into his signature pieces. An inspired choice for the thrusting steamer chairs, sofas, and chaises was wicker woven on the diagonal. Neither the shape nor the wicker treatment is static. Spectre turned to rattan for graceful chair silhouettes and bent table bases that embody his concept of eclipsing arcs and circles. "These pieces are perfect in all climates, in all seasons, in Palm Beach or Paris," says the designer, who even developed a wicker dog bed for his Scottie "Checkers."

Spectre's love of animals and admiration for the oeuvre of Diego Giacometti, with whom he shared a twenty-year friendship, resulted in another collection, entitled "Diego Mon Ami." Spirited interpretations of Giacometti's masterfully handcrafted iron animals frolic on small steel-and-glass side tables, rugs, porcelain, and lamps. This is Spectre's homage to a great talent.

As Spectre moved wicker indoors, he moved sophisticated lines and shapes outdoors with a lean, elegant series for Brown Jordan. In textiles, he reached back to a more glamorous age, with "Boogie Woogie" and "Jazz" sheet patterns, part of his program for Fieldcrest Cannon. You can feel the excitement of the Jazz Age, and the witty reference to Mondrian's famous painting by the same name. Boogie Woogie appears again in his electric rug for Louis De Poortere, S.A. And the polished chrome on his Art Deco–style lamps for Paul Hanson simply gleams.

Spectre's philosophy toward designing and buying furniture, just like his approach to decorating, hinges on eclecticism. His criterion is that every object in a room, from

Rattan dining room furniture. One of several collections produced in the Philippines, which Spectre visited to oversee production.

the art to the furniture, have its own integrity. Mixing these objects then, even if they are vastly different, will naturally yield elegant results because they transcend any stylistic differences. "We have no reason to be confined by anything," says Spectre. "It's like good taste. You can become a hostage to it. I've never felt you should not mix and experiment with furniture, with color, with metals, with art. You are only limited by your attitude. You can mix anything good as readily as you cannot." The contemporary yet classic pieces that form the core of the collection for Century (updated twice a year) and other manufacturers are each designed to be an individual element in any interior. This is true especially of his "Special Effects" group of tables, many with an Oriental look. "They complement all furniture, not just mine," says Spectre. Whether it is the "Okura Palace" table in an opulent lacquer finish or the sleek frosted-glass and polished chrome table, a "Special Effects" piece does just what the name implies: It makes a surprising style statement. "Furniture doesn't have to go with the house or even with the other furniture," affirms Spectre. "For houses that lack architectural features, furniture with strong design details can add dimension to an otherwise nondescript interior."

This sleek daybed in the Brown Jordan collection is built for outdoor use, but its fluid shape enhances interiors equally well.

Photographs courtesy Brown Jordan.

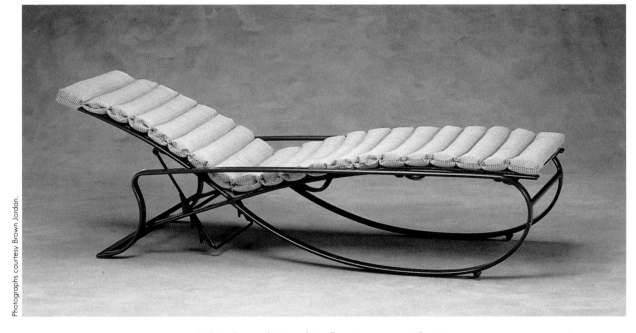

A chaise longue that paradoxically captures perpetual motion in a piece of furniture meant for relaxation.

The liquid lines of this bar trolley give it
the appearance of rolling in place.

The moment to take the cookies is when they pass the plate—
the Infamous New Canaan Cookie Company.

A twenty-first-century interpretation of the
bentwood rocker in aluminum.

Courtesy Louis de Poortere, S.A.

"Boogie Woogie" rug.

"Boogie Woogie" sheets.

Bold bed linens harkening back to the Art Deco thirties.

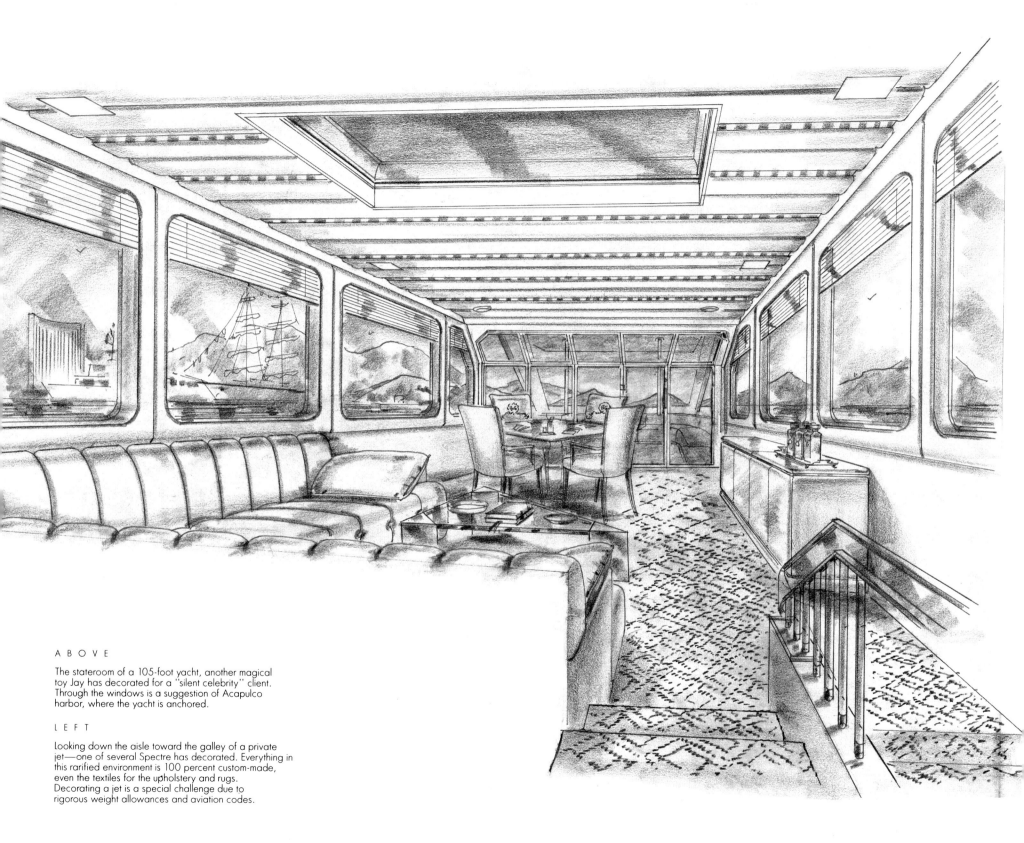

152

LEFT

The perceptive desk.
A signature piece in the
Perimeter collection,
it has a drop front
revealing four drawers.

RIGHT

The round Zodiac table
with metal base shown
in verdigris finish and
Zodiac icons etched
in the tabletop, with
Perimeter side chairs.

154

LEFT

A pair of ''Thin Man'' chairs, influenced by Dashiell Hammett's series, part of Spectre's 1991 Perimeter collection. The buffet and Zodiac mirror form part of Perimeter as well.

RIGHT

The Perimeter bed and night table. The fabric is from the Spectre collection of jacquards from Valdese.

What's the Angle? A witty side table with
a pullout tray with cork insert.

RIGHT

The Perimeter credenza in suede-colored primavera
with maple sides. Four fluted doors
conceal two compartments.

Geoffrey Bradfield with the design team.

Where is Spectre going next? It looks as though the sky's the limit. Eight designers, together with support staff, keep the phenomenal number of private commissions, commercial designs, and follow-up details running on time and on track. "We're definitely a team operation, with a common goal — to help people live beautifully and comfortably in an increasingly difficult world. And judging by our clients' response, we're succeeding."

List of Sources

Jay Spectre products may be purchased directly from the manufacturers through an interior designer.

Some stores featuring Jay Spectre designs for Century

Century Furniture Company
401 Eleventh Street NW
Hickory, NC 28603

Brown Jordan
9860 Gidley Street
El Monte, CA 91731

Brown Jordan
150 East 58th Street
New York, NY 10022

Louis De Poortere
240 Peachtree
Suite 4G2
Atlanta, GA 30303

Fieldcrest Cannon
1271 Avenue of the Americas
New York, NY 10020

Paul Hanson, Inc.
610 Commercial Avenue
Carlstadt, NJ 07072

Bloomingdale's
1000 Third Avenue
New York, NY 10022

Bloomingdale's
175 Bloomingdale Road
White Plains, NY 10105

Bloomingdale's
Chestnut Hill Mall
Newton, MA 02167

Bloomingdale's
20 Broad Street
Stamford, CT 06901

Bloomingdale's
Tyson's Corner Center
McLean, VA 22102

Bloomingdale's
White Flind
11305 Rockville Pike
Kensington, MD 20895

Bloomingdale's
The Falls
8778 SW 136th Street
Miami, FL 33176

Bloomingdale's
5840 Glades Road
Boca Raton, FL 33431

Bon Marché
3rd and Pine
Seattle, WA 98181

Macy's
760 Market Street
San Francisco, CA 94102

Neiman Marcus
1201 Elm Street #2700
Dallas, TX 75270

Hurwitz & Mintz
227 Chartres Street
New Orleans, LA 70130

Lazarus
7875 Montgomery Road
Cincinnati, OH 45236

Lazarus
Second and Main Streets
Dayton, OH 45401

Kaplan & Fox, Inc.
Boston Design Center
1 Design Center Place
Suite 200
Boston, MA 02210

Rich's Furniture Showroom
Interior Design Dept. #782/Furniture Dept. 83
4300 Ashford-Dunwoody Road NE
Atlanta, GA 30346

Rich's
1300 Cumberland Mall
Atlanta, GA 30339

Hubbuch's
324 West Main Street
Louisville, KY 40201